Hearts

That *Think*, *See*, and

Remember

The Qur'ān and the Secrets of the Spiritual Heart

Hearts

That *Think*, *See*, and *Remember*

The Qur'ān and the Secrets of the Spiritual Heart

EKRAM HAQUE

One
Humanity Under God

ISBN: 978-0-578-89716-5
Library of Congress Control Number:

Printed in Turkey

One Humanity Under God, Garland, TX

www.onehumanityundergod.com

Cover Design: Serhat Özalp

Editors:
Aaron Wannamaker
Kevin Miller

Arabic Transliteration Key

ء	o, ʿ	ر	r	ف	f
ا	ā, a	ز	z	ق	q
ب	b	س	s	ك	k
ت	t	ش	ū	ل	l
ث	th	ص	ṣ	م	m
ج	j	ض	ḍ	ن	n
ح	ḥ	ط	ṭ	ه	h
خ	kh	ظ	ẓ	و	w
د	d	ع	ʿ	ي	y
ذ	dh	غ	gh		

Table of Contents

Introduction

All praise and gratitude belong to Allāh, Who created the heart and illuminated it with faith. May He bless His Messenger, Muhammad ﷺ, to whom He revealed the Qur'ān and made it a cure for ailing hearts.

The idea that a heart can think, see, and remember is captivating, but with the Qur'ān as its advocate, it takes on an aura of certainty (*yaqīn*).

The Qur'ān says that a person's salvation in the Hereafter depends on the spiritual heart, not the physical heart that pumps blood. Hence, those who bring a pure heart (*qalbun salīm)* on Judgment Day will enter Paradise. As for this earthly life, the Prophet Muhammad ﷺ said a pure heart is a prerequisite for a healthy body.

The spiritual heart is the essence of our inner self, a repository of faith, God-consciousness, morality, and intentions. The heart is the master who orders the limbs to do its bidding.

Interestingly, other faiths and cultural traditions also recognize a spiritual or inner heart. Now science is joining believers' ranks, calling the heart a place of perception, emotion, and cognition. A heart has its own "brain" and a "magnetic field" that affects people around it.

Like its physical counterpart, the spiritual heart can become diseased and cause mortal harm. This book discusses the causes of the heart's major spiritual diseases and their cures.

Ekram Haque
April 11, 2021
Dallas, TX

Acknowledgements

I am immensely grateful to Allāh for inspiring me with this book's idea and enabling me to complete it. My countless thanks go to my wife, our children, and their spouses for giving me precious critiques. I sincerely appreciate Imam Arqum Rashid and Omar al-Ani for reviewing the manuscript and their invaluable input. This book also has enormously benefitted from Aaron Wannamaker and Kevin Miller's meticulous editing.

I am indebted to the publishers of *The Clear Qur'ān* for allowing me to use its thematic translation.

Finally, thank you, dear reader. I hope you will join me in exploring the secrets of the spiritual heart.

Foreword

The Qur'ān is *shīfā'* (healing) for the spiritually diseased hearts (10:57). Allah's Final Revelation to humanity tells us that the heart is the seat of faith, cognition, and moral decisions. The heart is a barometer of who we are. A pure heart will lead to salvation, and a corrupt heart will lead to damnation.

As an Islamic scholar and translator of the Qur'ān, I find its depiction of the spiritual heart fascinating, insightful, and deeply thought-provoking. One may not find a more comprehensive description of the heart's inner qualities in any other source.

This book takes a deep dive into the Qur'ān, the Prophet Muhammad's ﷺ Sunnah, and scholarly treatises to discover the secrets of the spiritual heart. Anyone interested in understanding why the heart occupies a central place in our lives will find this book invaluable.

Dr. Mustafa Khattab
Translator, The Clear Quran
April 11, 2021

Chapter 1

KNOW YOUR HEART

Have they not traveled through the land so their hearts may understand and ears hear; indeed, it is not the eyes that turn blind but the hearts in the bosoms that turn blind. – (Qur'ān 22:46)

The above verse refers to Mecca's idolaters, who rejected their prophet's message and mocked the idea of resurrection and divine punishment, even though scattered around them were remnants of nations whom Allāh[1] had destroyed for the same stubbornness. Although their eyes saw the ruins, their hearts remained blind to the truth because they lacked "insight."[2]

Growing up, I wondered why the Qur'ān almost always describes the human heart in spiritual or metaphysical terms. Could there be another dimension to the heart? If so, what was it, and how could I unlock its secrets?

---

1. The proper name for the Only Creator and the Supreme Being in the Arabic language is Allāh. Muslims believe that only the word Allāh encompasses the unique qualities of the Creator. Like Muslims, Arab Christians also refer to the Creator as Allāh. In this book, the author uses Allāh and God interchangeably to help Western readers, mindful that the term "God" is limited in its meaning.

2. *Tafsir ibn Kathir*, abridged, vol. 6, trans. Safiur Rahman al-Mubarakpuri (Riyadh: Darussalam, 2000), 592; Qur'ān 22:46.

From the Qur'ān's depiction, it is abundantly clear that the heart occupies the most important place in the body, surpassing even the mind. It is a piece of flesh where faith and intention reside, and emotions arise; it is a place of perception about right and wrong. A heart can be God-fearing or rebellious, kind or cruel, loving or hating, vengeful or forgiving, sad or happy. It has cognitive power, which, if harnessed, can lead its owner to the gnosis of the Creator; hence "he who knows himself knows God."[3] The heart has memory. No wonder the Qur'ān commands believers to "remember God profusely."[4]

If the heart has memory, one might ask what is the need to "remember" God? The answer is simple: Although God (Allāh) is hardcoded into our consciousness, we tend to forget Him because of external influences. Hence, remembering God in our hearts, reciting the Qur'ān, and glorifying Him on our tongues keeps us mindful of God.

Over 130 verses in the Qur'ān talk directly about the mystical nature of the human heart or *qalb*, not including 55 verses that refer to it with the alternative term *fu'ād,* or *ṣadr* (chest).[5] In Arabic, a *qalb* means something that turns or flips. Faith can increase or decrease depending on the heart's changing condition.[6] The Prophet Muhammad ﷺ [7] taught his

---

3. Ḥilyat al-Awliyā' 10/208.

4. Qur'ān 33:41.

5. "The human heart in the glorious Quran," The Quran Project, last accessed March 23, 2021, http://quranproject.org/The-human-heart-in-the-glorious-Quran-481-d. See also https://tanzil.net/.

6. Qur'ān 16:106.

7. Allāh commands Muslims to invoke His peace and blessings on the Prophet when the latter's name is mentioned. In Arabic it is acknowledged by "Sallallāhu 'Alayhī wa Sallam" and translated as God bless him and grant him peace. This book also uses the Arabic inscription ﷺ for that after the Prophet's name or mention.

followers a special prayer to beseech God: "O Turner of the hearts, keep my heart firm on Your religion."[8] This prayer is similar to Psalm 51:10: "Create in me a clean heart, O God; and renew a right spirit within me." A later chapter in this book, "Behind the Semantics," discusses the reason and the significance of the Qur'ān's use of different terms for the heart.

Although this book's primary focus is the Qur'ān's depiction of the spiritual heart, it also frequently uses the Prophet Muhammad's ﷺ sayings (Ḥadīth) and scholarly opinions to support or explain the verses of the Qur'ān. While the Qur'ān dwells almost exclusively on the spiritual heart, it does not reject the heart's physicality.

The Muslim scripture is not alone in its intense emphasis on the heart's spiritual persona. The Old and New Testaments also fiercely support the notion that the heart is the center of human emotions and intelligence. Proverbs 4:23 commands believers to "Watch over your heart with all diligence, for from it flow the springs of life." The Prophet Jesus ('Ēsa) reportedly said, "Blessed are the pure in heart, for they shall see God."[9] The Qur'ān says that people with a righteous heart will see Allāh on Judgment Day: *"On that day, some faces will be radiant, looking at their Lord."*[10] When the Prophet Muhammad's Companions asked him which people were the best, he replied, "Everyone who is pure of heart and sincere in speech.' They said: 'Sincere in speech, we know what this is, but what is pure

---

8. Tirmidhī, Ḥadīth #2140.

9. Matthew 5:8.

10. Qur'ān 75:21–22.

of heart?' He said: 'It is the heart that is pious and pure, with no sin, injustice, rancor or envy in it.'"[11]

Gautama Buddha suggested setting one's heart on doing good repeatedly, for it will fill the doer with joy. One Buddhist meditation technique is to "imagine as you breathe out that a warm light emerges from the center of your heart and touches the person you have in mind."[12]

Centuries of popular idioms and expressions about the heart tell us that the belief in its metaphysical qualities has been part of human existence across religions, times, places, and cultures. To this day, humans marvel at the wonders of the heart.

For example, someone's beloved is a sweetheart, a villain is evil-hearted, a parent is kindhearted, and a brave person is lion-hearted. The arrogant are hard-hearted, a sincere person tries wholeheartedly, a profound thank-you comes from the bottom of the heart, and a person feels it in his heart. Similarly, my friend had a "hearty" meal for which he expressed a "heartfelt" thanks. When asked where our heart is, most of us would point to our chest, but subconsciously we mean the heart inside that chest (*ṣadr*). We could go on.

The ancient Greeks believed a heart could perceive, and they called this ability *aisthesis*. Aristotle called the heart "the most important organ of the body" and "the seat of

---

11. Ibn Mājah, Ḥadīth #4216.

12. Thupten Jinpa, *A Fearless Heart: How the Courage to Become Compassionate Can Transform Our Lives*. (New York: Avery, 2015), 124.

"intelligence, motion, and sensation." Galen believed the heart to be "the organ most closely related to the soul."

Elsewhere in the world, the Persian polymath Ibn Sina (Avicenna) wrote that the heart is the "root of all faculties."[13]

In ancient Chinese medicine, the heart is where "*shěn*" or spirit resides, and the Mandarin Chinese language represents love, virtue, and thought with the heart's ideogram.

The view that the heart has metaphysical qualities is no longer limited to religious dogmas or popular folklore. New scientific research confirms that the heart has cognitive and emotional qualities. What neuropsychologists tell us today about the heart's inner capabilities is eye-opening. They contend that the heart has its own brain, called "heart-brain,"[14] and it mostly operates independently and sends far more signals to the brain in our head than the brain to the heart. I discuss the thought-provoking details in the chapters "The 'Spiritual' Heart in Science" and "Memories of the Heart" and compare them with the descriptions of the heart's capabilities in the Qur'ān.

Like its physical counterpart, the spiritual heart also becomes diseased. A ḥadīth[15] calls a spiritually pure heart a prerequisite for a healthy body. The Prophet ﷺ said, "Surely in the body is a lump of flesh which, if pure, then the whole body is pure, and if corrupt, then the whole body is corrupt.

---

13. "A History of the Heart," Standford.edu, last accessed March 23, 2021, https://web.stanford.edu/class/history13/earlysciencelab/body/heartpages/heart.html.

14. Exploring the role of the heart in human performance, https://www.heartmath.org/research/science-of-the-heart/.

15. A Ḥadīth is a saying of the Prophet Muhammad.

Truly, it is the heart."[16] A spiritually sick heart spells disaster. Later I will talk about the diseases of the spiritual heart and how to cure them.

16. Bukhārī, Ḥadīth #52.

Chapter 2

THE HEART AND THE QUR'ĀN

O humankind! Indeed, a warning from your Lord has come to you, a cure for what ails your hearts, and a guide and mercy for the believers. – (Qur'ān 10:57)

After Archangel Gabriel (Jibrīl) brought the first few verses of the Qur'ān to the Prophet Muhammad ﷺ, he tried to memorize it zealously until Allāh told him not to worry, for He would preserve the Qur'ān in the Prophet's heart ﷺ and teach him its interpretation.[17] As a sign of the heart's spiritual dimension and its domination of the human self, God revealed the Qur'ān onto the Prophet Muhammad's ﷺ heart, not his mind.[18] Hence, Muslims memorize the Qur'ān by heart. The Prophet's heart received the entire Qur'ān without any effort on his part. Another verse further assured him: "Verily, we *have revealed the Reminder [Qur'ān], and it is undoubtedly We Who will preserve it.*" [19] God fulfilled His promise of preserving the Qur'ān through writing

---

17. Qur'ān 75:16–19.
18. Qur'ān 2:97
19. Qur'ān 15:9.

and millions of *ḥuffāẓ (*sing. *ḥāfiẓ).* These are Muslims who have memorized the Qur'ān from cover to cover by heart. The memorization by heart is of greater significance because the *huffāẓ* can restore the Qur'ān if the written copies are lost. In the lifetime of the Prophet Muhammad ﷺ, the Qur'ān was primarily an oral tradition. Everyone memorized some portions of the Qur'ān while the scribes wrote down the revealed verses as the Prophet ﷺ dictated them.

In Islam, the heart's expanse is immeasurable. Therefore, it can encompass things no other organ can. According to mystics, God said, "the heavens and earth cannot contain me, but the heart of a believing person can."[20] God's greatest physical creation is His Throne, and even the Throne cannot contain Him because He is greater than His creation.

A prophetic tradition says, "Verily, Allāh has vessels among the people of the earth, and the vessels of your Lord are the hearts of his righteous servants. Of those the most beloved to Him are the softest and most tender of them."[21]

The Qur'ān is a reminder (*dhīkr*) and guidance from God Almighty. The more our hearts glorify Him, the more tranquil they become. The Qur'ān emphasizes this point in a chapter (*sūrah)* called "Thunder": *Surely hearts find rest in the remembrance of God."*[22] Like all hidden things, the restfulness of the heart is a feeling that one can only experience. When a heart is tranquil, its actions exhibit that.

---

20. Some claim that this is a prophetic statement, but the stronger opinion is that it came from Jewish narrations (Isrāēlīyāt). Muhammad Al- Ghazālī has quoted this in his Ihya 'Uloom Al-Deen, Vol. 3.

21. Musnad al-Shāmiyyīn, Ḥadīth #840; Nasiruddin Albani classified this narration as strong.

22. Qur'ān 13:28.

When we remember God frequently, our hearts become thankful in plenty and content in poverty. We do not become arrogant in richness because we know it is a bounty from God or become despondent when afflicted with calamity because we understand it is a test. The closer a heart draws to its Creator, the stronger and livelier it becomes. A cellphone's reception is best when closest to the cellular tower; the farther away it is from the tower, the weaker the signal becomes until it "dies." A heart that is bereft of God's remembrance becomes spiritually dead. Such a heart does not live to please its Creator but to pursue the lowly pleasures of life.

Like a living physical heart continually expands and contracts, a spiritual heart continuously experiences highs and lows, depending on the environment. According to an old saying, "a man is known by the company he keeps." Being among righteous people and in a favorable environment gives the heart a spiritual boost and positive reinforcement. A ḥadīth says, "A man is upon the religion of his best friend, so let one of you look at whom he befriends."[23]

> In a famous story from the Sīrah,[24] Ḥanẓalah ibn ʿĀmir, a Companion of the Prophet Muhammad ﷺ, came to him distressed, thinking he had become a hypocrite.[25] The Prophet ﷺ was surprised by Ḥanẓalah's statement, for he was among sincere Muslims. When asked why he thought so, Ḥanẓalah said his faith (*īmān*) was highest when in the

23. Tirmidhī, Ḥadīth #2378.

24. Seerah is a detailed biography of the Prophet Muhammad. In Islamic science, Seerah is a specialized genre distinct from Tafsir, Ḥadīth, and other branches of knowledge.

25. Theologically, a hypocrite (munafiq) is someone who outwardly proclaims Islam but inwardly is not a Muslim.

> Prophet's ﷺ company but suffered a decline when he became busy with family and work. The Prophet ﷺ told him that that was not a sign of hypocrisy, for if the fervor of Ḥanẓalah's faith remained the same as when he was in the Prophet's ﷺ company, the angels would shake his hands.[26]

The story of the two brothers helps illustrate this point further. The first spends time with a friend who owns a perfumery, while the second sits with someone who works as a blacksmith. The first brother returns in the evening, smelling like the fragrances sold at the store, whereas the second brother comes home smelling like coal. He also has smoke and soot on his face and clothes.

Just like the physical heart needs a balanced diet and exercise to be healthy, the spiritual heart relies on God's remembrance and worship for strength. Maintaining the spiritual health of the heart requires constant care and prayer. Hence, the Qur'ān teaches pious believers to pray, *"Our Lord, let not our hearts deviate after You have guided us to faith."*[27] This verse tells us that faith should not be taken for granted, for it can decline or be lost if we do not nurture and safeguard it. For those sincere to God, He will make their faith stronger.[28]

Undoubtedly, we all commit sins, and sins corrode our spiritual hearts. But if we repent and make amends, God removes the blemish of the sin, and our spiritual hearts thrive

---

26. This incident has been paraphrased. For the original version of this story, see Muslim, Ḥadīth #2750.

27. Qur'ān 3:8.

28. Qur'ān 48:4.

again. However, if we do not repent and commit more sins, our hearts become dark, cold, and hard.

In beautiful imagery, the Qur'ān describes the hearts of some Israelites as harder than a stone. *"Then your hearts became as hard as rock or even harder, for there are rocks from which streams gush forth; and, there are some that split open, and water flows out from them, while others fall in fear of God."*[29]

Let us examine the Qur'ān's similitude about splitting rocks through a famous waterfall. Every year, tourists flock to Niagara Falls on the border between Canada and the United States to view the grand waterfall. The majestic beauty of Niagara Falls awes the visitors, who snap countless photos of the beautiful scenery. Still, only a few reflect on the reality that the spectacular view would not have been possible if the rocks had not softened themselves to let the water pass.

History remembers the evil-hearted with disgust and the good-hearted with reverence. Pharaoh (Fīr'awn) is not the same as Moses (Mūsa); they are opposites. God promises salvation in the Hereafter to those who come with a pure heart (*qalbun salīm*), a heart that worships its Creator alone and acts righteously. A pure heart loves God above everything else and is full of mercy toward people. The Prophet Muhammad ﷺ said, "Verily, Allāh does not look at your appearance or wealth, but rather He looks at your hearts and actions."[30]

29. Qur'ān 2:74.

30. Muslim, Ḥadīth #2564.

God measures people's worth by their righteousness, which resides in the heart.[31] That's perfect justice, for the One Who created our shapes, colors, and social statuses cannot judge us on these things because we were born into them without our choice. However, He gave us power over our actions and showed us ways to purify our spiritual hearts with positive deeds. Then God inscribed His love in the pious hearts and endeared such hearts to the masses. The messengers, prophets, pious worshipers, and good-doers are the best examples of people whom humanity remembers with adoration, even though they were among the weakest and materially poorest. On the contrary, evildoers cause nothing but disgust in our hearts, even though they may wield immense power.

Our merciful God looks for tiny excuses to forgive us. He bestows ten rewards for one good deed and only one sin for an evil act to set us up for success. A ḥadith says the reward for one good deed can go up to 700. With this formula, it would take enormous sins to offset the advantage. Even then, God's mercy would look for the most negligible of excuses to pardon us.

A person's heart plays a central role in God's decision. To forgive, He looks for the intention, which resides in the heart. An action might appear wrong, but God will reward the doer because the intention was good. Conversely, He may reject a seemingly noble action because it stemmed from an evil intention in the heart. For example, a person's refusal to buy a car for his son might seem harsh, but it may be a good action if he knows his son is a reckless driver. Conversely, a person may

31. Riyad as-Salihin, Ḥadīth #234.

donate large sums of money, but God rejects his generosity because it stems from a desire to show off.

Since God alone knows what's in someone's heart, we must consider our intention before doing something. Using the same reasoning, we should refrain from hastening to judge others because of their outward actions. The litmus test for God's reward or punishment is what our hearts intended to do, not what our limbs ended up doing. The Qur'ān says that Allāh will not punish those who do something wrong mistakenly or due to forgetfulness.[32]

During the height of Muslims' persecution in Mecca (Makkah), 'Ammār ibn Yāsir, a young follower of the Prophet Muhammad ﷺ, uttered words of disbelief under the polytheists' vicious torture. The disbelievers had already tortured his mother to death. Full of remorse, 'Ammār came to the Prophet ﷺ and sought forgiveness for what he had said. The Prophet ﷺ asked him, "How did you find your heart when you said those words?" 'Ammār replied that his heart was firm in the faith. The Prophet ﷺ said, "When they do that to you again, you do the same." The Prophet ﷺ not only overlooked 'Ammār's infraction, but he also assured him and other Muslims that there was no problem with them saying negative things about Islam or the Prophet ﷺ under duress. The clear message here is that the intention in your heart is what matters.

A verse God revealed after this incident supported the Prophet's ﷺ position and exonerated 'Ammār, saying that

32. Qur'ān 2:286.

uttering words of disbelief under torture while the heart remained faithful was not a sin.[33] 'Ammār's story holds a practical lesson for us. In the aftermath of the 9/11 tragedy, we learned about the horrifying torture endured by Muslims in secret prisons worldwide. These prisoners are serving time without charge or due process. Under duress, they confessed to crimes they did not commit. Like 'Ammār, those who have given false, self-incriminating testimony under torture should know that God looks at their hearts. Because of the verse mentioned earlier, Muslim scholars agree that people undergoing oppression are permitted to proclaim disbelief to protect their lives. It cannot be called treason. Today's laws distinguish between evidence obtained freely and evidence acquired through coercion, the latter of which courts reject as inadmissible.

Interestingly, in Mecca, God declared criticizing Islam under torture blameless but in Medina (Madinah) deemed it blameworthy. The faith shone brightly in Mecca's persecuted Muslims' hearts despite their tongues expressing disbelief. On the contrary, in Medina, a group called the hypocrites (*al-munāfiqūn*) outwardly professed belief in Islam, but they rejected faith and harbored hostility in their hearts. God looked at the intention in their hearts rather than their outward actions in both cases.

33. Qur'ān 16:106.

Chapter 3

BEHIND THE SEMANTICS

"Do they not ponder over the Qur'ān? Had it been from anyone other than Allāh, they (the doubters) would have found many discrepancies in it." – (Qur'ān 4:82)

Why does the Qur'ān use three words for the heart: *qalb*, *fu'ād*, and *ṣadr*? We may also wonder why the Qur'ān uses many terms for Judgment Day, Paradise, and even for itself. To understand this, we need to delve into the Arabic language.

Linguists marvel at the enormously rich vocabulary of the Arabic vernacular. For example, the Arabs employed hundreds of words to describe a lion, such as *asad*, a fearless lion, *shibl*, a cub lion, *'abbās*, the strongest lion, *bāsil*, a fierce lion, *bahnas*, a prancing lion, and *ḥaydar*, a plump lion.

Arabs in the time of the Prophet Muhammad ﷺ loved poetic excellence and linguistic beauty. Their infatuation with the Arabic language's superiority, expressed mainly through oral traditions, caused them to call non-Arabs in neighboring lands *'ajam* (dumb).

The Qur'ān shocked and awed them with its far superior vocabulary and eloquence, challenging the pagan linguists to produce a single chapter like it and simultaneously telling them they could never do it. The Qur'ān's eloquence remains inimitable to this day.

Gabriel brought the Qur'ān to an Arab Prophet ﷺ whose people were at the apex of their mastery in poetry and flowery prose. The Qur'ān is not poetry, and the purpose behind its use of different words, phrases, and terminologies is not for show but rather to explain the reality of life to humanity and, ultimately, guide them to the Path of God. Explaining a subject using different words and angles ensures that people of all intellectual and educational levels can understand it. Each of the Qur'ān's words carries a unique connotation and special significance.

Some pagan Arabs admitted that, given its richness and eloquence, the Qur'ān could neither be the work of a human nor yet another form of poetry; still, they rejected the Prophet Muhammad's ﷺ message. Many other pagans, however, did call the Qur'ān poetry, fortunetelling, or magic, all accusations that Allāh refuted: *"And it is not the word of a poet; little do you believe. Nor the word of a soothsayer; little do you reflect. It is a revelation from the Lord of the worlds."*[34] The Meccan leaders hurled these slanders at the Prophet ﷺ. The Qur'ān denounced the disbelievers' statement that the revelation was nothing "*but evident magic.*"[35]

---

34. Qur'ān 69:41–43.

35. Qur'ān 34:43.

Qalb

Qalb is the primary word used in the Qur'ān for the physical and the spiritual heart. The physical heart continuously expands, contracts, and pumps blood through the body. And the spiritual heart struggles with faith and morality, courage and emotions, and good and evil. Therefore, the spiritual disease resides in the *qalb: "In their hearts (fī qulūbihim) is a disease,"*[36] *Qulūb* is the plural of *qalb*. Another passage says, *"The true believers are only those whose qulūb tremble at the remembrance of Allāh, and whose faith increases when His revelations are recited to them."*[37]

Another meaning of *qalb* is to switch something with another object. For example, one of the rules of the Qur'ān recitation is iqlāb because it switches the Arabic letter "n" (nūn) with "m" (mīm) if "n" comes before "b" (bā).

The word *qalb* can also mean something upside down. Arabs call one of their popular dishes *maqlūba* because after it is ready, they flip the pot over onto a dish and serve the contents upside down. However, in the spiritual context, the flipping of the *qalb* signifies its changing condition, not literally flipping.

Fu'ād

The word *fu'ād* comes from a root word that means "burning" or "inflamed." Overpowering emotions make our hearts feel inflamed or burning. Roasted meat is called *lahmun fa'eed*. When feelings of happiness, sadness, lust, frustration,

---

36. Qur'ān 2:10.

37. Qur'ān 8:2.

anger, or regret rise in our hearts, it is a *fu'ād,* and that is the context in which the Qur'ān uses this word. In the story of the Prophet Moses' childhood, his mother's heart became a *fu'ād* at the thought of Pharaoh finding out the truth: "*But there came to be a void in the fu'ād of the mother of Moses.*" [38] God had willed Pharaoh to select her as the wetnurse for Moses, unaware that she was the baby's biological mother. Now she obsessively worried that her cover would be blown. She calmed down only after God inspired her heart to trust that He would take care of the baby and her secret. At that point, the Qur'ān called her heart *qalb* because it no longer harbored extreme emotions.[39] Her heart was tranquil, accepting that no harm could touch her son. The Qur'ān says God will question the heart (*fu'ād*) on Judgment Day because when it sinned, it burned with emotions, passions, or lust.[40] In other words, it became a *fu'ād* from a *qalb.*

Ṣadr

When the Qur'ān refers to the heart as *ṣadr*, it means secrets or motives residing in it. Therefore, when Satan (*Shayṭān*) tries to entrap someone, he "*whispers in the ṣadr,*"[41] not their *qalb.* In the last chapter of the Qur'ān, God commands humanity to seek His refuge against Satan whispering in their *ṣudūr* (*sing. ṣadr*). When people conceal hatred, they do so in their *ṣadr.*

38. Qur'ān 28:10.

39. Qur'ān, ibid.

40. Amatullah, "The Heart: Fu'aad, Qalb and Sadr," Muslim Matters, Feb. 11, 2009, last accessed March 23, 2021, https://muslimmatters.org/2009/02/11/the-heart-fuaad-qalb-and-sadr/.

41. Qur'ān 114:5.

Because of this, the Qur'ān reminds them that *"Indeed Allāh is aware of what's in their ṣudūr."*[42]

Sometimes the Qur'ān uses *ṣadr* in the context of expanding someone's chest to increase their knowledge and understanding of religion. For example, *"Whomsoever God wishes to guide, He expands his ṣadr to Islam, and whomsoever He desires to lead astray, He makes his ṣadr tight as if he were climbing to the sky."*[43] In Chapter 94 of the Qur'ān, Allāh asks the Prophet Muhammad ﷺ a rhetorical question: *"Did We not expand your ṣadr?"*[44] Seerah books tell us that Gabriel cut open the Prophet's ﷺ *ṣadr* once in childhood when he lived with the wet nurse, Ḥalīmah, and another time in Mecca before the Ascension (*Mai'rāj*). On both occasions, Gabriel washed the Prophet's ﷺ heart to purify it and fill it with wisdom.

When God ordered the Prophet Moses to go to Pharaoh and speak with him, he prayed: *"My Lord! open up my ṣadr for me, and make my task easy."* [45] The Prophet Moses was afraid to confront Pharaoh and thought he needed inner wisdom and clarity to embark on the difficult task.

Some of the Qur'ān's commentators say the *ṣadr* is the external layer within which the *qalb* and *fu'ād* reside. When the ṣadr expands, what lies within it also expands. We learn that the *qalb* contains faith, *fu'ād* passions, and *ṣadr* secrets from the

42. Qur'ān 11:5.

43. Qur'ān 6:125.

44. Qur'ān 94:1.

45. Qur'ān 20:25–26.

preceding discussion.[46] The more one dives into the subtleties of the Qur'ānic vocabulary, the easier it is to understand why the Qur'ān challenged the greatest poets of seventh-century Arabia to bring a single chapter like it, the shortest of which is a mere three verses.

---

46. Sidi Abdullah Anik Misra, "What is the Difference Between the 'Heart' (Qalb), 'Kindling Heart' (fuaad), and the 'Pure Intellect' (lubb)?", Seekers Guidance, Nov. 4, 2009, last accessed March 23, 2021, https://seekersguidance.org/answers/general-counsel/what-is-the-difference-between-the-heart-qalb-kindling-heart-fuaad-and-the-pure-intellect-lubb/.

Chapter 4

THE DEVIL'S MISCHIEFS

O Children of Ādam, do not let Satan seduce you, just as he turned your parents out of the Garden. ... He and his tribe watch you from where you do not see them!" - (Qur'ān 7:27)

Any discussion of the heart's diseases inevitably leads to Satan (*Iblīs)*, our worst enemy. To ward off his ploys, we must understand his reality. Satan's interaction with humankind goes back to the creation of Adam (Ādam). Satan, whom God created before Adam, was visibly upset to see a potential rival in Paradise. It was hate at first sight, for at that point, Adam's body did not even have a soul, and Satan had no reason to detest him.

Satan's hatred of Adam, God's first prophet and father of humanity, intensified when he learned that God had elevated Adam and his progeny to be the best of His creation. To make matters worse, from Satan's perspective, God then asked Satan and the angels to prostrate to Adam—a command the angels obeyed while Satan refused and consequently incurred divine wrath.

In Islamic theology, Satan is from the *jinn*,[47] invisible creatures God created from the flames of "smokeless fire."[48] In Arabic, words made up of the letters *jīm* (j) and *nūn* (n) mean something hidden. Some other examples are *Jannah* (Paradise) and *janīn* (fetus). The concept of Satan in Christianity is that of a fallen angel. Like the jinn, angels are also invisible to humans, but God created them from light. Satan has free will, but angels don't, so they never disobey God. The Qur'ān says that Prophet Muhammad's ﷺ mission extended to jinns as well[49] and that among them are believers and disbelievers.[50]

The Qur'ān uses three main words for Satan: *Shayṭān* (nineteen times), *Iblīs* (eight times), and *Qarīn* (seven times). In Arabic, the word *Shayṭān* comes from *shayṭanah* (something far), so Satan's nature is farthest from any good; he is an irreconcilable and unrepentant enemy of God and humans. He will continue to disobey God and throw envy and sinful thoughts into people's hearts. Unlike Satan, humans repent when they fall into sin and disobey God, like the Prophet Adam and his wife, Eve, did and whom God forgave. In Islam, there is no such thing as "original sin." The Qur'ān explicitly says that "no person will bear the sins of others."[51] Muslims believe that all humans are born on their pure *fiṭrah* (innate nature), and only later in life do they choose their paths.

The name *Iblīs* comes from the Arabic verb *ablasa*, meaning "to despair." We learn from the Qur'ān that Satan lost all

47. Qur'ān 18:50.

48. Qur'ān 55:15.

49. Qur'ān 21:107.

50. Qur'ān 72:2.

51. Qur'ān 35:18.

hope of redemption when God cast him out of Paradise and decreed that his eternal abode would be Hell. Satan brought it upon himself, for he refused to repent and instead blamed God for his evil actions and vowed to disobey as long as he could. Besides divine wrath, Satan also suffers despair and defeat every day when believers refuse to follow his evil whispers.

The name *Qarīn* comes from the Arabic verb *qarana*, which means "to join." The pre-Islamic Arabs used this word in poetry. For example, the famous pre-Islamic odes, known as the *seven muʿallaqāt*, use *qarīn* to mean a constant companion. In a theological context, Satan is a *qarīn* because he always shadows humans to whom he whispers evil thoughts from birth to death. The Prophet ﷺ said, "Each one of you has a devil-companion from the jinn over him."[52] The term *qarīn* could also refer to angels that God has assigned to each person, but the angels only encourage their subjects to do righteous actions.

Decoding Satan's Plots

Satan, also called the devil, attacks subtly and retreats when a person remembers God. God allowed Satan some leeway over humans as part of divine wisdom, except over the most righteous among them. So, when Satan vowed, *"I will mislead them all,"* [53] God responded, *"But as for My devoted servants, you will have no authority over them."* [54]

52. Muslim, Ḥadīth #2814.

53. Qur'ān 15:39.

54. Qur'ān 17:65.

Before God expelled Satan from Paradise, condemned and accursed, he won a concession from Him to live on Earth until the end of time. Satan swore to use his long life to mislead Ādam's children into following his evil ways. A hadīth captures this dialogue thus: "Satan said: By Your might, O Lord, I will continue to mislead the children of Ādam, as long as their souls are in their bodies. The Lord said: 'By My might and majesty, I will continue to forgive them, as long as they seek My forgiveness.'"[55]

Many of us follow Satan without realizing it, for his attacks take the form of a whisper. Because of his ethereal and intangible shape, he can easily enter the human body. The Prophet ﷺ said, "Verily, Satan flows through the human being like the flowing of blood."[56] This ḥadīth may be a metaphor for Satan's ability to enter humans through the doors of doubts, desires, passions, and weaknesses.

Interestingly, Satan interacts with humans right from birth. A hadīth says, "No person is born but that Satan pricks him, and he cries from the touch of Satan, except for the son of Mary (Jesus) and his mother."[57] The Qur'ān tells us that Allāh protected Jesus and his mother from Satan's touch because of the supplication of Mary's mother: *"Verily, I seek refuge for her [Mary] and her offspring [Jesus]in You from the cursed Satan."*[58] In the Christian tradition, Satan did try to tempt Jesus, but this was later in life:

---

55. Muslim, Ḥadīth #91.

56. Muslim, Ḥadīth #2174.

57. Bukhārī, Ḥadīth #3248, Muslim, Haith #2366.

58. Qur'ān 3:36.

"The devil led him up to a high place and showed him all the kingdoms of the world in an instant. And he said to him, 'I will give you all their authority and splendor; it has been given to me, and I can give it to anyone I want to. If you worship me, it will all be yours.' Jesus answered, 'It is written: Worship the Lord your God and serve Him only.'"[59]

The Qur'ān says that Satan can try to interfere when a prophet wishes to guide his people: *"Whenever We sent a messenger or a prophet before you [O Muhammad], and he recited [Our revelations], Satan would influence [people's understanding of] his recitation. But eventually, Allāh would eliminate Satan's influence. Then Allāh would [firmly] establish His revelations. And Allāh is All-Knowing, All-Wise."* [60]

Satan has many tricks to deceive humans, and he approaches people according to their devotion to God. For those who embrace sin willingly, Satan overcomes them handily, but he employs more sophisticated ploys on the righteous. The Qur'ān says, *"do not follow the footsteps of Satan,"* [61] which, according to Suhaib Webb, an American scholar, indicates the multipronged way and the multiple levels on which Satan operates. Satan does not outright tell a believer to disbelieve, but instead, he acts subtly and gradually to lead them into sin and despair.

Two of Satan's biggest goals are to mislead people into disbelieving in God (*kufr*) and associating partners with Him (*shirk*), knowing they will be doomed forever if they die as

---

59. The Gospel According to Luke 4:5–8.

60. Qur'ān 22:52.

61. Qur'ān 2:208.

disbelievers or polytheists. As for believers who die having committed sins, they will eventually receive God's mercy.

Abdul Qādir Jīlāni,[62] an eleventh-century Muslim scholar and pious worshiper, said:

> Once I saw a dazzling light that filled the entire sky. Then a human frame appeared therein and said, "O Abdul Qādir, I am Lord, thy God. I have made everything prohibited lawful unto thee." I replied, "Get away from me, O Devil." As soon as I uttered these words, the luster in the sky turned into darkness, and the human frame began to fizzle out into smoke. Then I heard someone saying, "Abdul Qādir, I had misled seventy mystics with this device, but God saved you due to your knowledge and piety." To this, I rejoined, "No. It was simply a grace of God." After Abdul Qādir had related the incident, someone asked, "How did you know that it was Satan?" He replied, "Since he told me that he had made the things prohibited lawful for me."[63]

Abdul Qādir was alluding to an Islamic principle that God perfected the religion in the Prophet Muhammad's ﷺ lifetime, and no one can abolish its fundamental laws and obligatory rituals after him.

If we analyze the above incident, Satan's second attack was more powerful. Had Abdul Qādir accepted the insinuation

---

62. Full name Muḥyī-al-Dīn Abū Muḥammad b. Abū Sāleh ʻAbd al-Qādir al-Jīlānī (also Gīlānī).

63. Abu 'l-Hasan 'Ali al-Nadwi, "Shaykh Sayyid 'Abd al-Qadir al-Jilani," Hayat al-Ulama', January 17, 2013, last accessed March 23, 2021, https://hayatalulama.wordpress.com/2013/01/17/shaykh-sayyid-abd-al-qadir-al-jilani/.

that his knowledge had saved him from Satan's plot, he would have shown arrogance and earned God's wrath. Instead, by attributing his successful repulsion of Satan's attack to divine support, he directed praise to God, Who alone is worthy of it.

The incident also teaches us that no one is immune from the devil's plots. He incites arrogance in the pious by whispering that he is better than others, thereby destroying the person's good deeds, and incites despair in the sinner by whispering that there is no way Allāh will forgive him. No matter how big or many the sins, to think that Allāh cannot forgive a person is a far bigger sin. The Qur'ān and the Ḥadīth tell us the enormity of sin does not rule out Allāh's mercy for the penitent. In a verse that throws a lifeline to sinners and cold water on Satan, Allāh says, *"O My servants who have transgressed against themselves [by sinning], do not despair of the mercy of Allāh. Indeed, Allāh forgives all sins. Indeed, it is He who is the Forgiving, the Merciful. And return [in repentance] to your Lord and submit to Him before the punishment comes upon you; then you will not be helped."*[64]

The Prophet ﷺ reported that Allāh said,

> O son of Adam, so long as you call upon Me and ask of Me, I shall forgive you for what you have done, and I shall not mind. O son of Adam were your sins to reach the sky and were you then to ask forgiveness of Me, I would forgive you. O son of Adam, were you to come to Me with sins nearly as great as the earth and were you then to face Me, ascribing no partner to Me, I would bring you forgiveness nearly as great as it.[65]

64. Qur'ān 39:53–54.

65. Tirmidhī, Ḥadīth #34.

The Qur'ān and the Ḥadīth leave no doubt that there is salvation even for the most sinful person as long as they turn to God repenting.

The consequences of Satan's attacks are far more dangerous than human mischief. For example, dying from enemy fire in a just war will confer upon a Muslim martyrdom and earn him Paradise, but a defeat at Satan's hand may cause him to lose faith in God and suffer eternal damnation.

One of Satan's tactics is to portray evil as good. The Qur'ān says about the erstwhile nations of 'Ād and Thamūd that *"Satan had beautified for them their deeds, so he prevented them from the right way, even though they were people of insight."*[66] It is worth noting that Satan can trick people of "insight" if they reject faith or lower their guard. That was the case with Mecca's leadership in the early days of the Prophet's ﷺ mission. They admitted that the Prophet ﷺ was the most truthful and trustworthy in that society, yet they rejected his invitation to the One God and continued worshipping idols.

Satan also invites people to immorality,[67] intoxicants, gambling, sacrificing on stone altars for false gods, and fortune-telling. The Qur'ān calls them *"defilement from the work of Satan."*[68]

One of Satan's weapons is to incite humans to ungratefulness. In Adam and Eve's story, Satan tauntingly said

66. Qur'ān 29:38.

67. Qur'ān 2:69.

68. Qur'ān 5:90.

to God that most humans would not be thankful to Him.[69] What Satan said was not because he could foretell the future; it was merely a reaffirmation of God's decree, which states: *"Only a few of my servants are grateful."*[70] Perhaps he learned of this decree in Paradise before his expulsion. The logical way to counter Satan is to show constant gratitude toward God, Who has promised that the more we are grateful, the more He will give from His bounties.[71] Our hearts innately know their Creator alone is deserving of thanks (*shukr*) and praise (*ḥamd*). To do otherwise is to go against our Adamic nature.

Since we cannot see Satan while he can see us renders us vulnerable. Imagine the advantage an enemy would have over you if they could watch your every move while remaining invisible to you. Long before the invention of stealth bombers, Satan was attacking us stealthily.

On Judgment Day, Satan will absolve himself of peoples' misdeeds, saying, *"I had no authority over you, except that I invited you, and you accepted my call. So, do not blame me, but blame yourselves."*[72]

The Qur'ān and Sunnah teach how to keep Satan at bay or push him away when he attacks. A simple way is to say, preferably in Arabic, "I seek refuge in Allāh from the accursed Satan." In Arabic, the action of seeking God's refuge against Satan is called *ta'awwūdh*. The Qur'ān says, *"And before you recite the Qur'ān, seek refuge in Allāh from Satan the outcast."* [73] Scholars

69. Qur'ān 7:17.

70. Qur'ān 34:13.

71. Qur'ān 14:7.

72. Qur'ān 14:22.

73. Qur'ān 16:98.

explain that our weakness against Satan is that he sees us, but we don't see him. But when we recite *ta'awwūdh,* we attain the protection of Allāh, who sees Satan but Whom Satan cannot see. The *ta'awwūdh* dismantles Satan's advantage over humans.

Allāh orders believers to seek His protection in acts of worship and ordinary circumstances. For example, the five daily prayers start with *ta'awwūdh.* The Qur'ān says, *"If an evil suggestion comes to you from Satan, then seek refuge in Allāh. Indeed, He is all-Hearing and all-Knowing."*[74]

The Prophet ﷺ sometimes supplicated, "I seek refuge with Allāh, the All-Hearing, All-Seeing, from the accursed Satan, from his whisperings, evil suggestions, and insinuations."[75]

Satan runs away upon Allāh's mention because he fears Allāh, who he believes is the Lord of everything and the only One worthy of worship. In 2:34, when the Qur'ān calls Satan a "disbeliever," it means that Satan's disbelief comes not from disbelieving in the existence of God; instead, his disbelief comes from his rebellion against God's command. Satan's example also teaches us that arrogance can cause believers to act against their beliefs.

In the run-up to the Battle of Badr, Satan incited the Meccan polytheists to fight against the Muslims and promised to protect them, but he ran away fearful when defeat became imminent. The Qur'ān says, *"Satan made their deeds seem fair to them and said, 'None of the people shall prevail against you today; I shall*

---

74. Qur'ān 7:200.

75. *Tafsir Ibn Kathīr*, abridged, vol. 6, trans. Safiur Rahmān Mubārakpurī. (Riyadh: Darussalam, 2000), 688.

be your protector! But when the two forces fought each other, he turned on his heels, saying, 'This is where I leave you: I see what you do not, and I fear God. God is severe in His punishment.'"[76]

The Qur'ān and Sunnah prescribe a supplication (*du'*ā) for everyday life situations, from entering and leaving the house to eating and sleeping. There are even supplications to keep the devil's prying eyes from looking at our nakedness during bathing and using the restroom.

Even though Satan is persistent in his attacks, devoted believers can frustrate his nefarious designs. So the Prophet ﷺ said, "Verily, the believer will wear down his devils by obedience to Allāh, just as one of you wears down his camel on a journey."[77]

The last chapter of the Qur'ān is a powerful supplication against Satan:

> *"Say, I seek refuge in the Lord of humanity,*
> *the King of humanity,*
> *the God of humanity,*
> *from the mischief of every sneaking whisperer,*
> *who whispers into the hearts of people,*
> *from the jinn*[78]*and humans."* [79]

76. Qur'ān 8:48.

77. Musnad Ahmad, Ḥadīth #8717.

78. Qur'ān 4:76.

79. Qur'ān 114:1–6.

The last verse of the above supplication includes humans because some people manifest the traits of evil jinns. When we look at the deeds of the worst tyrants in history, we think they must be in league with the devil. How else could they perpetrate such horrors? Indeed, we know that some men and women not only imitate Satan in their actions but, worse, worship him. Satanism is the official religion of the Church of Satan,[80] and Satanic cults exist in many countries. Some of these cults may be less about worshipping the literal devil and more about living life according to Satanic beliefs like rejecting moral codes and rebelling against society.

People asked Ibn Ḥajar al-Haythamī, a medieval Muslim theologian, if there was a remedy for Satan's whispers (*waswasa*), and he said yes, to ignore them, and they would go away after a short time. However, if one pays attention to them and acts upon them, he said, the whispers will increase until they drive him insane or worse.[81] The Qur'ān says, *"Indeed, he [Satan] has no authority over those who have believed and rely upon their Lord."*[82]

While Satan has misled many and will continue to do so, his plots fail quickly in the face of God-conscious believers. The story of Abdul Qādir Jīlāni mentioned earlier is a case in point. The Qur'ān says, *"Indeed, the plot of Satan has ever been weak."*[83] Satan does not have the power to coerce people to sin, and he runs away when his victim remembers God. Knowing

80. https://www.churchofsatan.com/.

81. Ibn Hajar al-Haythami, Fatāwa al-Kubra al-Fiqhīyyah, Dar Sader, Beirut.

82. Qur'ān 16.99.

83. Qur'ān 4:76.

Satan's modus operandi helps in repulsing his attacks. His evil whispers disappear when believers invoke Allāh's help. But Satan is relentless, so warding off his attacks is a lifelong battle.

Reportedly Satan sent his workers to tempt the Prophet Muhammad's ﷺ Companions, but they kept coming back empty-handed. Irritated, Satan said, "What's with you?! Why are you unable to get anything out of them?" They replied, 'We have never seen people like these before.' Satan said, "Wait until worldly bounties open up for them, then you will be able to get what you want from them."[84] We infer from Satan's statement that excessive pursuit of worldly things makes us vulnerable to his attacks.

Although Satan is invisible to humans, Allāh has sometimes allowed the prophets and the righteous to see him. For example, the Prophet Muhammad ﷺ said, "Satan came in front of me and tried to interrupt my prayer, but Allāh gave me an upper hand on him, and I choked him."[85]

Allāh taught the Prophet ﷺ a beautiful supplication to ward off Satan and his disciples: *"Say, My Lord! I seek refuge with You from the whisperings of the devils. And I seek refuge with You, My Lord! lest they should come near me."*[86] While the addressee in this Qur'ānic verse is the Prophet Muhammad ﷺ, all believers should recite this supplication, for Allāh often teaches Muslims through the Prophet's ﷺ examples.

---

84. Ibn Abi al-Duniya in Makā'd al-Shaytān 60/39, quoted in *The Devil's Deceptions* by Imam ibn al-Jawzi, a translation of *Talbīs Iblīs* (Birmingham, UK: Dar as-Sunnah Publishers, 2014) 76.

85. Bukhārī, Ḥadīth #1210.

86. Qur'ān 23:97–98.

Imam Ibn al-Jawzī reported that Satan once came to the Prophet John the Baptist (Yaḥyā). Noticing Satan had many ropes on him, the Prophet John asked, "O Iblīs, what are these ropes I see on you?" Satan said, 'These ropes are the various lusts with which I strike the children of Ādam.' The Prophet John asked, 'Is there one for me, too?' Satan said, 'Yes, when you eat food to your fill, you experience weightiness, and it is for this reason you become disinclined to perform extra prayers, remembrance, and supplications.'"[87] The righteous prophet vowed he would never eat to his fill.

While Satan, our sworn enemy, unceasingly tries to tempt and mislead us, Allāh helps us through the angels, who whisper good thoughts to our hearts and protect us: *"For each one are successive angels in front and behind him who protect him by the decree of Allāh."*[88]

Some scholars say four angels accompany every person: the guardian angels in front and back, a recorder on the right, and a recorder on the left writing down everything we say and do.[89]

The Prophet ﷺ said, "Angels come to you in succession by night and day, and all of them get together at the time of the Fajr and 'Aṣr prayers. Those who stayed with you at night ascend to the Heavens, and Allāh asks them, though He knows everything about you well, 'In what state did you leave

87. Ibn Abi al-Duniya in Makā'd al-Shaytān 60/39, quoted in *The Devil's Deceptions* by Imam ibn al-Jawzi, a translation of *Talbīs Iblīs* (Birmingham, UK: Dar as-Sunnah Publishers, 2014) 70.

88. Qur'ān 13:11.

89. Qur'ān 50:17–18.

my slaves?' The angels reply: 'When we left them, they were praying, and when we reached them, they were praying.'"[90]

Angels are the allies of believers. They protect believers and whisper virtuous ideas into their hearts, and pray to Allāh for the believers' forgiveness. The Qur'ān mentions the supplication of a special group of angels:

> *"Those who carry the throne of God and those around it glorify their Lord with His praise and believe in Him. They ask for the believers' forgiveness, saying, "Our Lord, You embrace all things in mercy and knowledge. Forgive those who turn to You and follow Your path. Save them from the punishment of Hell and admit them, Lord, into the Eternal Garden You have promised to them, together with their righteous ancestors, spouses, and offspring; You alone are the Almighty; the All-Wise."*[91]

Another way Allāh helps is by giving us respite from Satan for an entire month. In a famous ḥadīth, the Prophet ﷺ said: "When the month of Ramaḍān begins, the gates of Paradise are opened, and the gates of Hellfire closed, and the devils are chained."[92] Ibn Ḥajar al-'Asqalānī, one of the commentators of *Bukhārī's Ṣaḥīḥ*, said that all the devils are chained except the one specifically assigned to a person.

Believers' hearts thrive during Ramaḍān due to fasting, extra prayers, charity, and abstention from backbiting and other vices. But they still have to contend with another

---

90. Bukhārī, Vol. 1, Book 10, Ḥadīth 530.

91. Qur'ān 40:7–8.

92. Bukhārī, Ḥadīth #1800, Muslim, Ḥadīth #1079.

powerful enemy that lurks within: the *nafs* or the lower self. In the next chapter, we will discuss this enemy's reality and how to defeat it.

Chapter 5

SOUL, SELF, AND THE HEART

"We created man, and We know the promptings of his soul and are closer to him than his jugular vein."
– (Qur'ān 50:16)

We cannot fully understand the role of the heart without knowing the soul. We learned in the preceding pages that the heart plays a pivotal role in human life, both physically and spiritually. But it does not act in isolation. The physical heart touches the entire body through the blood it pumps, and the spiritual heart affects our character and personality by its choices. But no heart can survive without the soul. So, what is the soul, and how does it interact with our heart?

The Meccan polytheists once asked the Prophet Muhammad ﷺ about the soul's reality. In the pre-Islamic days, Mecca was the center of idol worship, and the city's disbelievers could not have thought of asking about the soul. They were not people who delved into the deeper issues of human existence, but they had help from the Jewish community, the people of Torah, in formulating the questions. The goal was to test if their fellow citizen was indeed a prophet of God, as he claimed. The Prophet Muhammad ﷺ waited for a revelation to answer their question about the soul, and he didn't have to wait long. God sent down a verse of the Qur'ān that hints at the soul's reality but at the same time informs that, in His divine wisdom, the Creator of the soul has kept the details to Himself: *"They ask you [O Prophet] about the soul. Say: The soul is from the matters of my Lord, and you have been given little knowledge of it."*[93]

Because of this verse, only a handful of Muslim scholars have explored the soul's reality. Chief among those who have delved into this topic is Ibn al-Qayyīm al Jawzīyyah, whose seminal work, *Kitāb al-Rūḥ* (the Book of Soul), is an indispensable read on the subject. But whatever Ibn al-Qayyīm and others have written relies heavily on the Prophet's ﷺ explanation, for he also received revelation (*waḥy*) outside of the Qur'ān. Indeed, most details of Islam's worship rituals come from the Prophet's ﷺ statements, actions, and affirmations, collectively known as the *Sunnah*. Allāh supports the Prophet's ﷺ practices, whether directly based on the Qur'ān or of his own accord, calling the latter also God-inspired: *"He does not speak of his desire; it is a revelation revealed."*[94] This verse seals the Prophet's ﷺ authority as the chief explainer of the Qur'ān and Islamic laws.

So, what is the reality of this ethereal entity residing within us that we call the soul, spirit, or self? The Qur'ān uses two terms: *rūḥ*, which most scholars translate as "soul" or "spirit,"

---

93. Qur'ān 17:85.

94. Qur'ān 53:3–4.

and *nafs*, commonly called "self," the "lower self," or the "nature" of a human. In the Qur'ān, *rūḥ* and *nafs* appear 25 and 295 times, respectively. Most Muslim scholars consider *rūḥ* and *nafs* two names for the same thing. They use *rūḥ* when the body is without *nafs* and *nafs* when both are present in the body. Others say they are two different things: *rūḥ* is the pure spirit, and *nafs* is a person's desires and passions and can be good or bad.

Al- Ghazālī assigns two meanings to *rūḥ:* "a subtle body whose source is the cavity of the physical heart, and which spreads by the pulsative arteries to all the other parts of the body" and a "subtle and tenuous substance . . . which knows and perceives."[95] He ascribes several meanings to *nafs,* two of which he calls "the faculty of anger and desires" and the "reality" and "essence" of a person.[96] In pre-Islamic Arabic poetry, *nafs* referred to a person. The Qur'ān kept that connotation, as evidenced by several verses: "*Do not kill a nafs that Allāh has forbidden, except for a just reason*" (17:33). And "*It may be that you will kill nafsaka* (yourself*) in grief over them [O Prophet] if they do not believe in this message*"(18:6).

Rūḥ has other meanings, and it is one of the names of the Archangel Gabriel. For the topic in hand, we will focus on the *nafs* or the human lower self that includes blameworthy traits within every person, which we must strive to overcome. Earlier, we learned that a diseased heart suffers from doubts, desires, and envy, but these ailments emanate from the *nafs* or lower

95. Abu Hāmid Muhammad al-Ghazālī as quoted in *Ihya Ulum al-Din, Kitab Sharh 'Ajā'ib al-Qalb*, translated as *The Marvels of the Heart*, trans. Walter James Skellie. (Louisville: Fons Vitae, 2010), 28.

96. Ibid., 29–30.

self. It may be that the *nafs* acquires the blameworthy traits and projects them onto the heart.

The Qur'ān divides *nafs* into three types: 1) a*l-Nafs-al-'ammārah,* a commanding self that pushes toward sin and evil, 2) *al-nafs al-lawwāmah,* a self that reproaches a sinner; and 3) *al-nafs al-muṭma'innah,* a tranquil self that is content with God's decree in all circumstances.

Al-Nafs-al-'Ammārah appears in the Qur'ān in the story of the Prophet Joseph (Yūsūf), who pushes away the sexual advances of his master's wife, 'Azīz. He was in the prime of his youth and extraordinarily handsome. On top of that, he was a domestic slave in that lady's house, and, therefore, refusal was hardly an option. But Allāh helped him, and he sprinted toward the door to escape the evil invitation, saying, "*I seek refuge in Allāh! Indeed, He is my Lord! He made my living in great comfort! Indeed, the wrongdoers will never be successful.*"[97]

Allāh called the young Joseph His sincere servant. As mentioned earlier, Satan cannot misguide those who sincerely worship Allāh with all their heart. A while later, when the Prophet Joseph's innocence became official, the woman admitted: "*And I do not acquit myself. Indeed, the lower self is a persistent enjoiner of evil, except for those upon whom my Lord has mercy.*"[98] Some say Joseph said this, but the context does not support this opinion. Instead, it seems that the admission of guilt came from the Prophet Joseph's master's penitent wife. Scholars say that *al-nafs-al-'ammārah* is a commanding self. It

97. Qur'ān 12:23.

98. Ibid, verse 53.

overtakes its victims as few things do, and its antidote is plenty of remembrance of Allāh. Many men and women have at least once in their life felt a sudden, overpowering urge to sin, so powerful that they found it almost impossible to shake off. Without controlling *al-nafs-al-'ammārah,* one risks falling into heedlessness where sins do not perturb them anymore. Because bad company fuels the lower self, the Qur'ān warns against obeying those who excessively pursue their desires and are lost.[99]

Allāh uses *al-nafs al-lawwāmah* as an oath (*qasam*): *"And I swear by the reproaching soul."* [100] The context is the Day of Resurrection, with Allāh assuring the deniers of today that it will undoubtedly happen. The verse's tone indicates that it is not just a promise but also a threat to disbelievers that Allāh will resurrect their crumbled bones on that day, and they will stand before Him to answer for their deeds. Allāh calls this type of self *nafs al-lawwāmah*, or the reproaching self, because it rebukes sinners for their infractions and coaxes them to repent.

Most believers fall into this category, for they occasionally commit sins but are neither heedless nor the most righteous. When they commit sins, it bothers them, and they do not rest until they seek Allāh's forgiveness and return to doing good deeds. Their penitent heart will qualify them for God's mercy. The Qur'ān says whom God would admit into Paradise will be those *"Who feared the Most Merciful without seeing Him, and came with a repenting heart."*[101] A reproaching self aspires for nobility and

99. Qur'ān 18:28.

100. Qur'ān 75:2.

101. Qur'ān 50:30.

keeps trying despite tripping and falling short. The Prophet ﷺ said, "By Him in whose hand my soul is, if you did not sin, Allāh would replace you with people who would sin, and then they would seek forgiveness from Allāh, and he would forgive them."[102]

The most virtuous type of self is *al-nafs al-muṭma'innah*, the tranquil and content self which belongs to the righteous. On the Day of Judgment, Allāh will say: *"O al-nafs al-muṭma'innah, return to your Lord, well-pleased and well-pleasing; join now the ranks of My righteous servants, and enter My Paradise."*[103] Such a self is the hallmark of God's messengers and prophets and believers who have certainty of faith, those who do not waver or doubt in the most trying situations. They not only refrain from sin; they also do not desire sin. They are like a group of people about whom the Qur'ān says, "*Allāh has endeared the faith to you and has made it pleasing in your hearts and has made hateful to you disbelief, defiance, and disobedience. These are indeed the rightly guided.*"[104]

The Qur'ān tells us that God will admit into Paradise untold numbers of believers from the followers of all His prophets, including Abraham (Ibrāhīm), Moses, Jesus, and Muhammad.

Because the self is hardcoded in our being, its effect on the heart is constant. Our righteous and self-reproaching selves uplift our hearts by waging *jihād* (struggle) to overcome evil, but our lower selves degrade the heart through sin.

---

102. Muslim, Ḥadīth #2749.

103. Qur'ān 89:27–30.

104. Qur'ān 49:7.

Interestingly, the term *jihād* applies more to our inner struggles with the self, particularly with the lower self, than to the outer struggles of war. The West misconceives *jihād* as "holy war," even though such terminology does not exist in Islamic Sharīʿah. Because of the wrong definition of *jihād* in Western writings, few know that the word in Islam means striving or exerting the utmost effort to do something. Therefore, we can extrapolate that *jihād* also means striving against our lower self's evil inclinations.

One of the meanings of *jihād* is fighting in an armed conflict for a just cause, which is honorable; all nations recognize the notion of a "just war." This type of *jihād* is not perpetual, like *jihād* against the self. A person cannot struggle for good externally if they fail in the struggle against the inner self. Allāh promises excellent rewards for waging *jihād* against the *nafs*: *"But as for the one who feared standing before his Lord, and restrained his lower self from the evil desires, then surely Paradise will be their abode."*[105]

The Prophet ﷺ called *jihād* against the *nafs* the highest form of *jihād*. He said, "The one who strives in *jihād* is he who strives against his lower self."[106] When the Prophet ﷺ was returning from a military expedition, he said, "We now return from the *jihād asghar* (small struggle) to *jihād akbar* (big struggle)." His Companions asked, 'O Prophet of God, what is *jihād akbar?*' He replied, "The struggle against the *nafs.*"[107]

105. Qur'ān 79:40–41.

106. Tirmīdhī, Ḥadīth #1621.

107. See, for example, Abū Bakr Aḥmad Ibn al-Ḥusayn al-Bayhaqī (d. 485 H), *Kitāb al-Zuhd al-kabīr*, ed. ʿĀmir Aḥmad Ḥaydar, (Beirut: Mu'assasat al-Kutub al-Thaqāfiya, 1996), 165, no. 373.

Ibn al-Qayyim said, "The most compulsory form of *jihād* is *jihād* against the ego; against unbridled passions; against the Devil, and against being worldly."

Taming the *Nafs*

> *By the soul and the One Who fashioned it, then inspired it to understand right and wrong, he who purifies it will indeed be successful, and he who corrupts it will surely fail.* – (Qur'ān 91:7–10)

The above verses tell us several things. First, God has inspired our souls to distinguish between right and wrong. Second, with God-given consciousness, it is up to us whether we choose salvation or destruction. Third, the successful will be those who purge their *nafs* of vice, ego, passion, and sinful tendencies, and the doomed will be those who will let their lower selves' passions run amok. Implied in these verses is the message that God gave us a test and told us how to pass it, and now the rest is up to us. Finally, the self's purification (*tazkiyatun nafs*) follows the same path as the heart's purification (*taṭhīr qalb*). The heart and the self are inseparable companions.

In Islam's fourteen centuries and among the nations of previous prophets, those who subjugated and disciplined their lower selves were the ones who refused to listen to their desires. They trained themselves to ask before every desire: "Do I *need* it or merely *want* it?" We are safe if we only seek what we need, but we put ourselves on a slippery slope when we chase things out of the lower self's greed. The former state is praiseworthy: *"And whoso is saved from the covetousness of his nafs, such are successful."*[108] In another place, the Qur'ān calls those who purify their souls *successful* and those who corrupt it *doomed*.[109]

Some scholars contend that a *nafs* that is greedy is also miserly. Such a person wants everything for himself without wanting to share it with others. When the Prophet Muhammad ﷺ and his followers migrated to Medina, the local Muslims (*Anṣār*) welcomed them with an outpouring of love and, in some cases, offered half of their wealth to their immigrant brethren (*Muhājirūn*). Some of the *Anṣār* were themselves needy, but they gave precedence to the immigrants who had arrived from Mecca with only the clothes on their backs. Allāh praises their love and self-sacrifice in the Qur'ān: *"Those already settled in the city and firmly rooted in faith, love those who migrated to them for refuge, and harbor no desire in their hearts for what has been given to the latter; they give them preference over themselves, even if they too are needy."* [110]

Before doing something, some early Muslims asked, "Will my action please Allāh or displease Him?" As the old maxim goes, prevention is better than cure. Perhaps they thought, why do something blameworthy now and rectify it later? Why not do it right from the start? This strategy should help a God-conscious person drop an evil plan and, in case of a virtuous plan, check his intention that he is doing it to please God, not his *nafs*. We can apply this self-examination to all actions:

108. Qur'ān 64:16.

109. Qur'ān 91:9–10.

110. Qur'ān 59:9.

"Should I say this, watch this, listen to it, touch it, or gaze at it?" In most cases, the self, which God inspired to distinguish right from wrong,[111] will provide the answer. It will help against the lower self, which whispers to go with the flow, blend in with the popular culture and flashy lifestyle, and impress others.

If we suppress our lower self, the higher self will take over our decisions. A tamed lower self shuns rebellious and unrighteous behavior. God's messengers weakened the lower self so that it became docile and compliant. Their diligence rendered it harmless. That happened when they suppressed the covetous demands of their lower selves. The Prophet Muhammad ﷺ fasted over six months in a year and praised the Prophet David's (Dāwūd) fasts and prayer, which he said were most beloved to God.[112]

The Prophet ﷺ disliked eating his fill, calling a full belly the worst of vessels. Therefore, he said, "the son of Adam cannot fill a vessel worse than his stomach, as it is enough for him to take a few bites to straighten his back. If he cannot do it, he may fill it with a third of his food, a third of his drink, and a third of his breath."[113]

According to a ḥadīth, the Prophet ﷺ "would spend several nights in a row with an empty stomach, and his family would not find anything for dinner."[114] The hunger pangs that the Prophet ﷺ suffered were not due to his inability to provide for himself and his family. As the head of state, he could eat

111. Qur'ān 91:8.

112. Bukhari, Ḥadīth #3420.

113. Tirmidhī, Ḥadīth #2380.

114. Tirmidhī, Ḥadīth #2360.

the best food, but he saw a full stomach as detrimental to the pursuit of spiritual excellence. Indeed we know how a big meal makes us lazy and slack in worship.

At the time of his death, the Prophet's ﷺ possessions consisted of some mats, blankets, jugs, a bowl from which he ate, and other simple things even though he was the ruler of Arabia.

To clarify, hardly anyone can emulate the Prophet's ﷺ examples of abstaining from the self's pleasures; he set the bar too high. However, we can at least aspire to achieve it.

The lower self thrives in an environment of *ghaflah* (heedlessness), where people think they need to binge on food and sensual pleasures. To them, living a successful life is synonymous with self-gratification since, in their eyes, this is the only life they have anyway. For disbelievers, the resurrection is *ba'īd,* literally far, but in this context, not a possibility. When warned of life after death and accountability, they mocked the Prophet ﷺ, saying there was no way "*when we are dead and have become dust*" that God will resurrect us? "*That is a far return,*"[115] meaning nearly impossible.

Remembering death can be an excellent check for the *nafs*. The Prophet ﷺ called the death "the destroyer of pleasures" and urged us to remember it often.[116] When we visit a cemetery and pass through rows upon rows of graves, we unmistakably understand the reality of death. These people, like us, walked upon the earth, some living for a hundred years, but death

115. Qur'ān 50:3.

116. Tirmidhī, Ḥadīth #2307.

eventually brought their world to an end. Looking at previous civilizations' remnants, we marvel at their architecture and history, but where are they now? Although they have moved on, God's angels have recorded their actions for the Day of Reckoning: *"We shall indeed bring the dead back to life, and We record what they send ahead and what they leave behind. We have recorded everything in a Clear Book."*[117]

Death will catch up one day no matter how rich, powerful, or famous a person. Knowing that *no one* can delay or hasten death shows us that *someone else* controls our lives and death. Such a realization should humble people and compel them to accept the existence of a higher being and the futility of their arrogance. The Qur'ān says, *"And every nation has its appointed term; when their term comes, they can neither delay it nor hasten it by a single moment."* [118]

Before a major court hearing, defense lawyers strategize how to defend their clients against the charges. They analyze every possibility from every angle, leaving no stone unturned. What then of defending before the Judge of all judges where no lawyer shall be allowed and where the witnesses will be our own limbs. The angels will place before us our *book* containing the minutest details of our lives. Then a caller will say, *"Read your book. Today you are enough to judge yourself."*[119] Sinners will scream in grief: *"Woe to us! What kind of book is this that leaves nothing small or great except that it has recorded it?"*[120]

---

117. Qur'ān 36:12.

118. Qur'ān 7:34.

119. Qur'ān 17:14.

120. Qur'ān 18:49.

Our book of deeds is like an autobiography with one difference: the angels write this book, not us, but our actions determine what they write. These scribes are God's representatives assigned to each of us during our worldly life. They and we are inseparable. Only at death do we part.

So, here is an important point. It is up to us to decide what the book contains. The faithful and dutiful scribes only record our deeds without fear or favor, and this book will not be subject to alteration or revision. The question is, aren't we all writing our book?

The Qur'ān also tells us that the righteous will receive their book from the right side in the right hand and happily show it to their family on a day that is the crowning moment for all their life's work. They will be elated, and why not? They have made it unscathed to the eternally blissful abode where they will no longer suffer pain, stress, trials, sickness, or death. The book is akin to a report card without any prejudice or bias from the preparer.

The angels will hand the book to the unrighteous from the left side and in the left hand. Fear will overtake them, and they will wish their evil deeds could be separated from them and thrown away to a far-flung place. They will have failed the test. God will say, *"This Book of Ours speaks about you in truth. Indeed, We were having your actions transcribed."*[121]

As we can see, the book of deeds will be a witness for or against us, and we must decide what to write in it.

---

121. Qur'ān 45:29.

Recognizing that we are constantly under God's watchful gaze acts as a powerful deterrent against evil actions and a stimulus for righteous actions. For example, Abu Bakr, the closest friend of the Prophet Muhammad ﷺ, said he felt shy when undressing for a bath, knowing that even in that state, he was in the knowledge of God.

The Qur'ān repeatedly reminds humankind that this world and its enjoyments are fleeting, and *real* life is that of the Hereafter. So, no one should shortchange the superior pleasures of eternity by indulging in unrighteous behavior, pursuing this inferior world's unlawful yet short-lived joys. Muslims, Christians, and Jews agree that human life began in Paradise, where our parents, Adam and Eve, the first humans, lived in unparalleled splendor. But then they erred and were sent down to an imperfect world where, unlike Paradise, there was no royal treatment for them and where they had to strive to survive. However, God promised Adam and Eve's children that He would admit them back into Paradise if they did well on earth. It is a fascinating thought: our ancestral home was Paradise, and now we should direct all our efforts toward returning to that everlasting and blessed abode.

The Prophet ﷺ said, "Take advantage of five before five: your youth before your old age, your health before your illness, your riches before your poverty, your free time before your work, and your life before your death."[122]

It is profound advice and deserves a voluminous commentary, which the scope of this book does not permit.

---

122. Mukhtasar Shu'ab Al-Iman lil Bayhaqi, Ḥadīth #9575.

On Judgment Day, those who did not use their faculties and privileges for positive things will regret it, but it will be too late. Even those in Paradise will have remorse for not working harder, which would have entitled them to a loftier place.

'Umar Ibn al-Khaṭṭāb, one of the Prophet's ﷺ close companions, used to say, "Take yourself to account before you are taken to account (*ḥāsibū anfūsakūm qabla an tūḥāsabū . . .*)."[123] In today's parlance, we call it self-evaluation. There are two types of people. The first are those who do not know their weaknesses. As a result, they get angry when told of their shortcomings and may never get rid of them. The other type consists of those who rebuke themselves for their mistakes and, when told of one they did not know, thank the person for showing them the mirror.

Our *nafs*, like the heart, can aspire to righteousness or heed the call of its basest instincts. It can be a force for tremendous good or abject evil, and our own choices in life will dictate which way our *nafs* inclines. If we surround ourselves with positive ideas, good company, lawful earnings, a chaste lifestyle, and honesty, our *nafs* will reach the level of *al-nafs al-muṭma'innah*, the persistently content self. The possessor of *al-nafs al-muṭma'innah* pleases God and inspires fellow humans. In the opposite case, the *nafs* becomes rebellious and a scourge for its possessor and society.

One of the best ways to keep the *nafs* in check and help it to purify itself is to love God and be conscious of Him with all our hearts and soul. When we love Him, He will guide us, and

---

123. Aḥmad Ibn Ḥanbal (d. 241 H) as quoted in *Kitāb al-Zuhd Kabir*, ed. Muḥammad 'Abd al-Salām Shāhīn (Beirut: Dār al-Kutub al-'Ilmiyya, 1999), 99, no. 633.

if He guides us, our hearts and ourselves will want to do what pleases Him. And when He is pleased with us, He will suffice for us. The Qur'ān promises: "*Whoever is conscious of Allāh, He will make a way out for him and provide him from where he does not even imagine. And whoever places his trust in Allāh, He is sufficient for him.*"[124]

124. Qur'ān 65:2–3.

Chapter 6

THE "SPIRITUAL" HEART IN SCIENCE

"Indeed, in the creation of the heavens and the earth; the alternation of the day and the night; the ships that sail the sea for the benefit of humanity; the rain which Allāh sent from the clouds to revive the earth after its death; the scattering of creatures throughout, and the shifting of the winds and the clouds drifting between the heavens and the earth—in them are surely signs for people of understanding." – (Qur'ān 2:164)

The preceding chapters leave no doubt that religions and cultures throughout history have always considered the heart the center of faith and spirituality, a place of emotion, perception, and cognition, and the director of our actions. On the other hand, science has generally viewed the heart as merely a blood pump that sustains life, ignoring the heart's other personas. Science's reductionist view is divorced from reality and has garnered much-deserved criticism. Stephen Harrod Buhner has some harsh words for scientists who dismiss the spirituality of the heart. He calls the scientific community's attitude "a particular form of imperialism," accusing them of stealing "from all of us the historical recognition of the heart as an organ of perception" and substituting it with "a mechanical heart and the belief that the brain is the only organ capable of thought."[125]

Buhner calls the brain "merely an organic computer" without "inherent moral nature" and warns that the continued "training of children in a system of perception that is amoral leads to behaviors in adults that have no moral basis."[126]

Despite mainstream science's indifference toward the heart's cognitive capabilities, growing scientific data indicates that the scientific community increasingly recognizes its perceptive side.

New scientific research on the heart astounds us with its findings and shows us that the gulf between the two worldviews is narrowing. While mainstream science may not call the heart a *spiritual* organ, it has admitted that it has a metaphysical dimension. If we look beyond semantics, we will find that science confirms, in its vernacular, certain spiritual qualities of the heart that, for centuries, religions believed in and preached.

This chapter aims to share some scientific findings and compare them with the religious, particularly Islamic, concept of the spiritual heart and how to keep it healthy.

Scientific discoveries that the heart has emotion, courage, and wisdom, among other qualities, are mostly confined to

---

125. Stephen Harrod Buhner, *The Intelligence of the Heart in the Direction Perception of Nature (The Secret Teachings of Plants)* (Rochester, VT: Bear & Company, 2004), 118.

126. Ibid.

psychophysiology and neuro-cardiology, so perhaps it will take decades before they become widely accepted.

According to the HeartMath® Institute, a nonprofit research organization,

> The heart is, in fact, a highly complex information-processing center with its own functional brain, commonly called the heart brain, that communicates with and influences the cranial brain via the nervous system, hormonal system, and other pathways. These influences affect brain function and most of the body's major organs and play an important role in mental and emotional experience and the quality of our lives.[127]

That concept of the heart governing the "quality of our lives" is similar to the ḥadīth of the Prophet Muhammad ﷺ, quoted earlier, that says a pure heart is the guarantor of a healthy body. Spiritually speaking, whether a person is good or evil depends on his heart, not his mind. We know that the mind does not help make moral choices, but the heart does.

Henry David Thoreau, the nineteenth-century American naturalist, essayist, poet, and philosopher, said, "The intellect is powerless to express thought without the aid of the heart."[128]

---

127. Rollin McCraty, *Science of the Heart: Exploring the Role of the Heart in Human Performance*, vol. 2 (Boulder Creek, CA: HeartMath Institute, 2015), 2.

128. Henry David Thoreau, "On the Art of writing," American Transcendentalilst Web, last accessed March 23, 2021, https://archive.vcu.edu/english/engweb/transcendentalism/authors/thoreau/hdt-art.html.

The research also shows that the heart has a "magnetic field which radiates outside the body, carries information that affects other people and even our pets, and links people together in surprising ways."[129] How often have we realized that the company we keep shapes our personality and is a barometer of who we are? Being around people affects us, even if subtly. From experience, we know that some people make us cheerful, and we feel at peace in their company, while others make us feel agitated and put off. In other words, our hearts have different experiences around different people.

Traditionally, scientists have focused on how the heart responds to the brain's commands. However, new research shows that communication is two-way between the heart and brain, with each organ influencing the other's function. The heart communicates with the brain in four significant ways: 1) neurologically (through the transmission of nerve impulses), 2) biochemically (via hormones and neurotransmitters), 3) biophysically (through pressure waves), and 4) energetically (through electromagnetic field interactions)."[130]

The pioneering research of physiologists John and Beatrice Lacey, done in the 1960s and 1970s, influenced behavioral medicine and neuroscience.[131] The couple's cutting-edge work and others' work after them showed that the heart has an independent nervous system ("the brain in the heart"). It interacts with the brain in two-way communication, sending

129. Ibid.

130. Ibid.

131. J. Richard Jennings and Michael G.H. Coles, John I. Lacey, A Biographical Memoir, Biographical Memoirs, vol. 88 (Washington, DC: National Academy of Sciences, 2006).

more information to the brain than the brain sends to the heart.[132]

As the Laceys' research progressed, they discovered that the heart behaved "as though it had a mind of its own," and when it sent messages to the brain, "the brain not only understood but also obeyed."[133]

We now know that the heart's rhythm is not monotonous but continuously fluctuating. Such findings align with an Islamic prayer that says, "O Turner of the heart, make my heart steadfast on Your religion." Our hearts sometimes feel inspired and happy and, at other times, depressed and unmotivated. Our hearts can go through many emotions that affect our faith's vibrancy on a single day.

Another significant finding about the heart is that the heart's "brain" or intelligence works "independently of the cranial brain to learn, remember, make decisions, and even feel and sense."[134] We can now say that religion is not alone in saying that the heart "remembers, decides, and feels." We may also contend that there is a scientific basis too for saying "I remembered God in my heart," "my heart decided to do this," or "I felt something wrong in my heart."

The heart is also known to produce hormones that affect cognition and tolerance, trust and friendship, motivation and

---

132. Rollin McCraty, Science of the Heart: Exploring the Role of the Heart in Human Performance, vol. 2 (Boulder Creek, CA: HeartMath Institute, 2015), 5.

133. Ibid, 4.

134. Ibid, p. 5.

behavior, and enduring love. These hormones affect a mother's bonding with her child during childbirth and lactation.[135]

The way we live has a profound impact on our hearts. Positive thinking and emotions help the heart stay healthy, whereas stress and negative emotions lead to numerous physical diseases.[136]

Hope, optimism, and positivity are our lifelines, and they are among humankind's most beautiful traits. Religion and science agree on these virtues' positive effects on our lives, sometimes for different reasons. Those who do not possess them live an existence of cynicism, doubt, and depression.

Today, from boardrooms to classrooms across America, we hear how important it is to be positive. Psychologists and self-help gurus tell us how indispensable these qualities are for a happy and meaningful life.

Fourteen centuries ago, Islam told humanity never to despair of God's mercy and to thank Him even in adversity because one may find ease in life's difficulties. God puts bumps in the road of one's life to forgive them for some shortcoming,

---

135. G. Telegdy, G., "The action of ANP, BNP and related peptides on motivated behavior in rats," *Reviews in the Neurosciences*, vol. 5, no. 4 (1994): 309–315. See also J. Gutkowska, J., et al., "Oxytocin is a cardiovascular hormone," *Brazilian Journal of Medical and Biological Research*, vol. 33, n. 6 (2000): 625–633.

136. D. S. Goldstein, "Stress, allostatic load, catecholamines, and other neurotransmitters in neurodegenerative diseases," *Cellular Molecular Neurobiology*, vol. 32, no. 5 (2011): 661–666. See also M. Frese, "Stress at work and psychosomatic complaints: a causal interpretation," *Journal of Applied Psychology*, vol. 70, no. 2 (1985): 314; J. Gaines and J. Jermier, "Emotional exhaustion in a high stress organization," *Academy of Management Journal*, vol. 26, no. 4 (1983): 567–586; and B. Fowers, "Perceived control, illness status, stress and adjustment to cardiac illness," *Journal of Psychology*, vol. 128, no. 5 (1994): 567–579.

shower them with mercy, or make things easier. For example, the Qur'ān says that God embeds relief in every difficulty.[137]

When Pharaoh and his army caught up with the Israelites, some, seeing imminent death, told the Prophet Moses, *"We are sure to be overtaken."*[138] The great prophet responded with certainty, *"No, surely my Lord is with me. He will guide me."* [139] And for all to see, His Lord did guide him. So the Prophet Moses and his people crossed the Red Sea, which God parted for them, while Pharoah and his marauding band drowned.

In his Sermon on the Mount, the Prophet Jesus saw optimism in poverty, hunger, grief, and persecution. As God's messenger, he looked past the pessimism of the moment and reminded people of God's promise of help for the poor and the persecuted, who endure suffering patiently.

The Qur'ān urges believers to be patient in adversity because Allāh is with those who are patient (*ṣābirūn*).

Some scientific studies show compelling evidence that the heart is attached to a field of information free from the classical limits of time and space.[140] The heart has intuition and processes information about a future event before it happens.[141]

---

137. Qur'ān 94:5–5.

138. Qur'ān 26:61.

139. Ibid. 26:62.

140. R. McCraty, M. Atkinson, and R. T. Bradley, "Electrophysiological evidence of intuition: Part 1. The surprising role of the heart," *Journal of Alternative and Complementary Medicine*, vol. 10, no. 1 (2004): 133–143.

141. Ibid., 325–336.

A ḥadīth says, "Beware of the intuition of the believer. Verily, he sees with the light of Allāh."[142] So we may describe intuition (*firāsah*) as an insight, gut feeling, inspiration, or light that God puts in the heart of some of His servants.

The year the Prophet Muhammad ﷺ died, he said to his youngest daughter, Fāṭimah, that his death might be near, saying, "Gabriel recited the Qur'ān unto me and I unto him once every year, but this year he has recited it with me twice. I cannot but think that my time has come. Verily, you will be the first of the people of my house to meet me."[143] As it turned out, Fāṭimah died six months later, the first of his kin to depart after him.

Throughout history, cultures, and religious traditions, people have understood the heart as the source of love, wisdom, intuition, and courage. Hence we hear the expressions "put your heart into it" or "speak from the heart." According to the HeartMath® Institute study cited earlier, "Such expressions reflect what often is called the intuitive, or spiritual heart," something akin to a person's "inner voice, soul or higher power . . ."

Scientists sometimes associate emotions, thoughts, and intuitions with the "energetic heart" because they cannot measure, touch, or see something that operates in a covert

---

142. Tirmidhī, Ḥadīth #3127.

143. Bukhārī, Ḥadīth #3376.

domain and therefore is not subject to direct observation.[144] Physicist David Bohm describes it as "our implicate order and undivided wholeness."[145]

Finally, the heart generates the most extensive rhythmic electromagnetic field of all the organs, approximately 100 times stronger than the brain. The electromagnetic field influences those sitting up to three feet from a person. The organized patterns of energy from the heart, as Buhner points out, directly affect organisms' functioning outside the heart.[146] When people meet, they transfer energy and information through the electromagnetic fields of their hearts.[147] It is something that modern instruments can measure with increasing accuracy.

144. K. H. Pribram, *Brain and Perception: Holonomy and Structure in Figural Processing* (Hillsdale, NJ: Lawrence Erlbaum Associates, Publishers, 1991). See also E. Laszlo, *Quantum Shift in the Global Brain: How the New Scientific Reality Can Change Us and Our World.* (Rochester, VT: Inner Traditions, 2008); E. Mitchell, "Quantum holography: a basis for the interface between mind and matter," in *Bioelectromagnetic Medicine*, ed. P.G. Rosch and M.S. Markov (New York: Dekker, 2004): 153–158; W. A. Tiller, J. W. E. Dibble, and M. J. Kohane, *Conscious Acts of Creation: The Emergence of a New Physics.* (Walnut Creek, CA: Pavior Publishing, 2001): 201–202.

145. D. Bohm and B. J. Hiley, *The Undivided Universe* (London: Routledge: 1993).

146. Stephen Harrod Buhner, *The Intelligence of the Heart in the Direction Perception of Nature (The Secret Teachings of Plants).* (Rochester, VT: Bear & Company, 2004): 91.

147. Ibid., 109.

Chapter 7

MEMORIES OF THE HEART

"Remember your Lord in your heart with humility and reverence in a moderate voice, morning and evening. And do not be one of the heedless." – (Qur'ān 7:205)

The word "remember" (وَاذْكُرْ / *wadhkūr*) appears 292 times in the Qur'ān in 14 derived forms.[148] Depending on the context, it can also mean "remind," "mention," "admonish," or "take heed." One of the names of the Qur'ān itself is *adh-Dhīkr*, "the Reminder." So, where does the memory of a person reside? Since the Qur'ān focuses on the spiritual heart, one would deduce that that is the place of human memory. For example, Allāh revealed the Qur'ān onto the Prophet Muhammad's ﷺ heart, we memorize something by heart, and we remember God in our hearts.

---

148. "Quran Dictionary," Corpus Quran, last accessed March 23, 2021, http://corpus.quran.com/quarandictionary.jsp?q=*kr. This is an open source project. The Quranic Arabic Corpus is available under the GNU public license with terms of use.

On the other hand, science tells us that human memory forms and resides in various parts of the brain: the hippocampus, the neocortex, and the amygdala. Moreover, the memories are of different types. "Episodic memory" (memories of specific events in our lives, like the coffee we had with a friend) comes from the hippocampus. "Implicit memory," such as motor memories, comes from the basal ganglia and cerebellum. "Short-term working memory" comes from the prefrontal cortex.[149]

Interestingly, "cellular memories" reside in every cell, including the intrinsic cardiac nervous system, home to "both short-term and long-term memory functions."[150]

An article titled "Organ Transplants and Cellular Memories"[151] contends that "it is not uncommon for memories, behaviors, preferences, and habits associated with the donor to be transferred to the recipient." The article's lead author, Dr. Paul Pearsall, Ph.D., received numerous awards for his research on the interworking between the brain, heart, and immune system. In addition, his groundbreaking research on heart transplant recipients inheriting their donors' memories led to the formation of Cleveland Clinic's new Heart/Mind program.

Because of the prevailing assumption that learning mainly belongs to the nervous system and secondarily to the immune

---

149. "Where are memories stored in the brain?", Queensland Brain Institute, last accessed March 23, 2021, https://qbi.uq.edu.au/brain-basics/memory/where-are-memories-stored.

150. Rollin McCraty, Science of the Heart: Exploring the Role of the Heart in Human Performance, vol. 2 (Boulder Creek, CA: HeartMath Institute, 2015), 5.

151. "Organ Transplants and Cellular Memories," Paul.Pearsall.com, last accessed March 23, 2021, https://www.paulpearsall.com/info/press/3.html.

system, many researchers doubt that the recipients of heart transplants can experience personality changes, paralleling the personalities of donors they have never met.[152] They argue that personality change would only result from the "effects of the recipients' immunosuppressant drugs, psychosocial stress, and pre-existing psychopathology."[153] The idea that the recipient can mimic the donor's traits appears far-fetched to them.

Dr. Pearsall and his team cite other studies that show that "all living cells possess memory and 'decider' functional subsystems within them."[154] They argue that "the recent integration of systems theory with the concept of energy . . . provides compelling logic . . . that all dynamical systems store information and energy to various degrees."[155]

This chapter discusses two cases of heart transplant recipients who exhibited aspects of their donors' personalities. Dr. Pearsall and his coauthors provide multiple other examples in their report, which this space does not allow (citation at the end of case 2). Around the world, tens of thousands of people go through life with the aid of someone else's heart beating

---

152. Ibid..

153. D. T. Lunde, "Psychiatric complications of heart transplants," *American Journal of Psychiatry*, vol. 126, no. 3 (1969): 1190–1195. See also W. F. Kuhn et al., "Psychopathology in heart transplant candidates," *Journal of Heart Transplants*, vol. 7, no. 3 (1988): 223–226 and F. M. Mai, "Graft and donor denial in heart transplant recipients," *American Journal of Psychiatry*, vol. 143, no. 9 (1986): 1159–1161.

154. J. G. Miller, *Living Systems*. (New York, NY: McGraw-Hill, 1978).

155. G. E. Schwartz, L. G. Russek, "Dynamical energy systems and modern physics: Fostering the science and spirit of complementary and alternative medicine," *Alternative Therapies in Health Medicine*, vol. 3, no. 3 (1997):46–56. See also G. E. Schwartz, L. G. Russek, "Do all dynamical systems have memory? Implications of the systemic memory hypothesis for science and society," in *Brain and Values: Is a Biological Science of Values Possible?*, ed. K. H. Pribram. (Hillsdale, NJ: Lawrence Erlbaum Associates, 1998) and G. E. R. Schwartz, L. G. Russek, "The origin of holism and memory in nature: The systemic memory hypothesis," *Frontier Perspectives*, vol. 7, no. 2 (1998): 23–30.

in their chests, and many of them can corroborate Pearsall's observations.

Case 1

A sixteen-month-old boy named Jerry had drowned in a bathtub. The recipient was a seven-month-old boy named Carter. The donor's mother, a physician, noted:

> The first thing is that I could more than hear Jerry's heart. I could feel it in me. When Carter first saw me, he ran to me and pushed his nose against me and rubbed and rubbed it. It was just exactly what we did with Jerry. Jerry and Carter's heart is five years old now, but Carter's eyes were Jerry's eyes. When he hugged me, I could feel my son. I mean, I could feel him, not just symbolically. He was there. I felt his energy.
>
> I'm a doctor. I'm trained to be a keen observer and have always been a natural-born skeptic. But this was real. I know people will say that I need to believe my son's spirit is alive, and perhaps I do. But I felt it. My husband and my father felt it. And I swear to you, and you can ask my mother, Carter said the same baby-talk words that Jerry said. Carter is six, but he was talking Jerry's baby talk and playing with my nose just like Jerry did.
>
> We stayed with the . . . [recipient family] that night. In the middle of the night, Carter came in and asked to sleep with my husband and me. He cuddled up between us exactly like Jerry did, and we began to cry. Carter told us not to cry because Jerry said everything was okay. My husband and I, our parents, and those who really knew Jerry have no doubt. Our son's heart contains much of

> our son and beats in Carter's chest. On some level, our son is still alive.

When the researchers interviewed the recipient's mother, her story corroborated the statement of the donor's mother. Here is what she said:

> I saw Carter go to her [donor's mother]. He never does that. He is very, very shy, but he went to her just like he used to run to me when he was a baby. When he whispered, "It's okay, mama," I broke down. He called her "Mother," or maybe it was Jerry's heart talking. And one more thing that got to us. We found out talking to Jerry's mom that Jerry had mild cerebral palsy, mostly on his left side. Carter has stiffness and some shaking on that same side. He never did as a baby, and it only showed up after the transplant. The doctors say it's probably something to do with his medical condition, but I really think there's more to it.
>
> One more thing I'd like to know about. When we went to church together, Carter had never met Jerry's father. We came late, and Jerry's dad was sitting with a group of people in the middle of the congregation. Carter let go of my hand and ran right to that man. He climbed on his lap, hugged him, and said, "Daddy." We were flabbergasted. How could he have known him? Why did he call him dad? He never did things like that. He would never let go of my hand in church and never run to a stranger. When I asked him why he did it, he said he didn't. He said Jerry did, and he went with him.

Case 2

Carl, a thirty-four-year-old police officer was fatally shot attempting to arrest a drug dealer. The recipient was a fifty-six-year-old college professor, Ben, who suffered from heart disease.

The donor's wife reported:

> When I met Ben and Casey [Ben's wife], I almost collapsed. First, it was a remarkable feeling seeing the man with my husband's heart in his chest. I think I could almost see Carl in Ben's eyes. When I asked how Ben felt, I think I was really trying to ask Carl how he was. I wouldn't say that to them, but I wish I could have touched Ben's chest and talked to my husband's heart.
>
> What really bothers me, though, is when Casey said offhandedly that the only real side-effect of Ben's surgery was flashes of light in his face. That's exactly how Carl died. The suspect[156] shot him right in the face. The last thing he must have seen is a terrible flash. They never caught the guy, but they think they know who it is. I've seen the drawing of his face. The guy has long hair, deep eyes, a beard, and this real calm look. He looks sort of like some of the pictures of Jesus.

156. The original word has been changed to "suspect" due to the spiritual theme of this book.

The recipient, Ben, reported:

> If you promise you won't tell anyone my name, I'll tell you what I've not told any of my doctors. Only my wife knows. I only knew that my donor was a 34-year-old, very healthy guy. A few weeks after I got my heart, I began to have dreams. I would see a flash of light right in my face, and my face gets real, real hot. It actually burns. Just before that time, I would get a glimpse of Jesus. I've had these dreams and now daydreams ever since: Jesus and then a flash. That's the only thing I can say is something different, other than feeling really good for the first time in my life.

Casey, the recipient's wife, reported: "I'm very glad you [the researcher] asked him about his transplant. He is more bothered than he'll tell you about these flashes. He says he sees Jesus and then a blind flash. He told the doctors about the flashes but not Jesus. They said it's probably a side effect of the medications, but God, we wish they would stop."[157]

In both cases, it seems evident that the donors' hearts had memories of people and incidents that, after the transplant, the recipients exhibited. For example, in the first case, the child receiving the heart recognized the donor's father and called him "Daddy," and rubbed his nose against the nose of the donor's mother, just like her deceased child used to do.

---

157. "Organ Transplants and Cellular Memories," Paul.Pearsall.com, last accessed March 23, 2021, https://www.paulpearsall.com/info/press/3.html.

In the second case, the recipient continued to see Jesus in his dreams, followed by hot flashes, the last things the donor had encountered before being killed. The hot flashes signified the bullet that struck him in the face, and Jesus represented the calm face of the killer, who looked like Jesus's depiction in popular images.

In light of the above cases, several questions come to mind. How does one's heart remember life experiences? Does a person's heart see what his eyes see? If not, do the eyes somehow transfer the images they see to the heart? In the Qur'ān, we find an indirect reference to the heart's confirmation of what eyes see: "*The heart did not lie in what he saw.*"[158] The verse refers to the Prophet Muhammad's ﷺ seeing Angel Gabriel in the latter's original form during *Maiʿrāj*. The Prophet's ﷺ heart believed what his eyes saw, even though seeing the greatest angel was intensely magnificent.

158. Qur'ān 53:11.

Chapter 8

FAITH, INTUITION, AND INNER LIGHT

> *"Is he whose chest Allāh has opened to Islam and follows a light from his Lord [like the heedless]? So woe unto those whose hearts are hardened against the remembrance of God! They are in manifest error."* – (Qur'ān 39:22)

The Qur'ān makes it clear that faith is a light that God has placed deep inside the hearts of those He chooses. Faith, therefore, is the enlightenment of the heart and the biggest favor of God. In His perfect knowledge and justice, He gives it to some and withholds it from others: *"And whoever God wants to guide, He expands his breast to Islam."*[159]

With vibrant faith, one can surmount all difficulties without falling into despair. A person of faith is more likely to be an optimist who sees the glass as half full rather than half empty. All religions teach their adherents to think positively and to be hopeful. Modern scientific studies show that hope,

159. Qur'ān 6:125.

positivity, and optimism hasten recovery and improve patients' quality of life. Someone with no optimism may succumb to depression and despair. They may see life as meaningless after a tragedy and, in extreme cases, consider suicide. The number of suicides mounted during the 2007–2008 financial crisis.[160] Ironically, some of those who committed suicide were still millionaires, despite steep stock market losses, when they took their lives.

Prophet Jacob called despair a sign of disbelief. While still reeling from the loss of Joseph over 30 years ago, news came of Benjamin's detention in Egypt. Instead of sinking into hopelessness, the Prophet Jacob said, "*O my sons, go and seek news of Joseph and his brother. Do not despair of God's mercy; none despairs of God's mercy except the unbelieving people.*" [161] Despite facing heartbreaking tragedies, the Prophet Jacob hoped he would find Joseph and Benjamin, and he connected that hope to his faith in God.

Several studies have suggested that religious faith and prayer improve mental health and well-being. Spirituality can reduce stress, which helps strengthen the immune, endocrine, and cardiovascular systems. According to several studies and experiments, people of faith recover faster from depression, grief, and anxiety disorders. Allāh has made anxiety an innate part of creation: "*Indeed, humankind was created anxious.*"[162]

---

160. Feifei Sun, "Financial Suicides," *Vanity Fair* (April 2009), https://www.vanityfair.com/news/2009/04/financial-suicides.

161. Qur'ān 12:87.

162. Qur'ān 70:19.

But then He sent the Qur'ān as "*a guidance and healing for the believers*."[163] The recitation of the Qur'ān calms the heart.

In his article, "Research on Religion, Spirituality and Mental Health: A Review," Dr. Harold G. Koenig cites hundreds of studies that support the premise that patients who have religiosity and spirituality recover faster from mental, psychological, and psychiatric illnesses than those who lack faith. Koenig, a psychiatry professor at Duke University Medical Center, said people with religious attachment had relatively lower incidents of depression, suicide, anxiety, and substance abuse.[164]

According to Dr. Michael T. Murray, a leading authority on natural medicine, "It is medically irresponsible not to include a spiritual dimension in a patient's plan for treatment and recovery."[165]

In a 1996 *USA Today* poll of 1,000 American adults, 79 percent of the respondents said that spiritual faith and prayer could help people recover from disease, and 63 percent thought that physicians should talk to patients about spiritual faith and prayer.[166]

One of the men who helped promote the healing power of prayer was Larry Dossey, MD, author of the best-selling *Healing Words: The Power of Prayer and the Practice of Medicine*

---

163. Qur'ān 41:44.

164. Harold G. Koenig, "Research on Religion, Spirituality and Mental Health: A Review," *Canadian Journal of Psychiatry* (2008).

165. Michael T. Murray, *What the Drug Companies Won't Tell You and Your Doctor Doesn't Know*. (New York: Simon & Schuster, 2009), 33.

166. Ibid.

and *Prayer Is Good Medicine*. Dr. Dossey analyzed 4.3 million published scientific reports, of which 364 were on faith or religion. Although the numbers are small, the implications are eye-opening: prayer and religious commitment promote good health and healing.[167]

Because of the numerous scientific studies describing the positive effects of faith and spirituality on healing, the American College of Graduate Medical Education now requires all psychiatry residents to be trained on religious or spiritual factors that influence psychological development.

We can say that the light of faith comes with intuition (*firāsah*), knowledge (*'ilm*), and wisdom (*ḥikmah*). The stronger one's faith, the stronger these qualities will likely be. It is because God has hardwired the consciousness of right and wrong in us. A pure heart naturally inclines toward and embraces good while dissociating from and rejecting evil. When we smell something fragrant, we take a deep breath to savor the pleasant aroma, but we hold our breath in the face of a foul smell, which we find repulsive.

Wābiṣah ibn Mā'bad, a Companion of the Prophet Muhammad ﷺ, went to him to ask some questions that had concerned him. As he reached the Prophet ﷺ, he found a group already sitting around him. When Wābiṣah came close, the Prophet ﷺ said, "Have you come to ask about righteousness and sin?" Surprised, Wābiṣah said yes. The Prophet ﷺ gently struck Wābiṣah's chest and said, "Ask your soul, ask your heart, O Wābiṣah. Righteousness is what

---

167. Michael T. Murray, ND, and Joseph Pizzorno, ND, *The Encyclopedia of Natural Medicine*, (New York: Atria, 2012), 22.

reassures your soul and your heart, and sin is what wavers in your soul and tenses up your chest, even if people approve it in their judgments again and again."[168] Given that the heart has its own "brain" that perceives and decides, it makes complete sense to *ask* the heart.

Ḥārith al-Muḥāsībī, a ninth-century Iraqi scholar, said: "In many matters, the ultimate jurist is the heart. This is why it is so important to try to constantly purify our hearts, for the greater the degree of the heart's purity, the more a person is inclined naturally towards the truth."[169]

The Prophet's ﷺ statement means the heart is a guide, and we should listen to it as long as it guides us aright. But a heart tempted by Satan could prompt one to do evil, in which case we must reject the heart's whims. The very consequence of sin and evil is that it eats away at the heart's ability to guide us.

"And do not follow your desire," says the Qur'ān because *"it will lead you astray from the way of Allāh."*[170]

How does a heart receive intuition, knowledge, and wisdom? To this question, we can say that some matters pertain to the metaphysical world. They are intangible. We cannot touch or see them, but we can experience them. God grants intuition, knowledge, and wisdom to whom He wishes. God says in the Qur'ān, *"And We certainly gave Luqmān wisdom."*[171]

---

168. Dārimī, Ḥadīth #2533.

169. Ḥārith al-Muḥāsībī, Risāla al-Mustarshīdīn (Treatise for the Seekers of Guidance) transl. Zaid Shakir (Hayward, CA: NID Publishers, 2008), 91.

170. Qur'ān 38:26.

171. Qur'ān 31:12.

The Prophet Muhammad ﷺ once prayed that God would grant ʿAbdullāh ibn ʿAbbās, his young cousin, a deep understanding of the religion. Ibn ʿAbbās was in his teens when the Prophet ﷺ died, but within a few years, he became the greatest exegete of the Qur'ān after the Prophet ﷺ.

When Abu Bakr ibn Quhāfah was about to die, he told his daughter, ʿĀyeshah, about her "two sisters." ʿĀyeshah was surprised, as she only had an older sister, Asmā. Through inner knowledge, Abu Bakr knew that the child his other wife, Habibah bint Kharijah, was carrying in her womb was a daughter, which she delivered after his death.[172]

Omar, who succeeded Abu Bakr, once shouted during a Friday sermon in Medina, "O Sāriyah, move to the mountain!" People were perplexed. Sarīyah ibn Zanīm was the commander of a Muslim army fighting in Persia, far away from Medina. When the expedition returned, Sāriyah said, "O Commander of the Believers! We were defeated when we met our enemy, but then we heard a voice calling, 'O Sāriyah! Move to the mountain!' We moved to the mountain and turned our backs to it, and then we defeated them."[173]

Abu Hāmid Muhammad al-Ghazāli, or Imam al-Ghazālī, said in his masterpiece *Iḥyā' ʿulūm al-dīn* (*The Revival of Religious Sciences*) that a famous mystic named Abu Sa'īd al-Kharrāz told him:

172. Muwaṭṭā, Book 36, Ḥadīth #36.33.40.

173. Reported by Imam Ahmad in "Fadā'il Al-Sahābah," Abu Nu`aym in "Dalā'il Al-Nubuwwah," Al-Diya' in his "Al-Muntaqa min Al-Masmu`at", Ibn 'Asākir in his "Tārīkh," Al-Bayhaqy in "Dalā'il Al-Nubuwwah," and Ibn Hajar in "Al-Isābah" with a good chain of narration.

> I entered the sacred mosque and saw a poor man wearing two tattered cloaks, and I said to myself, "This man and his ilk are a burden upon mankind." But he called me to him and said, "Allāh knows what is in your heart, so beware of Him." Then I asked forgiveness of Allāh secretly, at which he again called me and said, "It is He Who accepts repentance from His servants." Then he disappeared from me, and I did not see him again.[174]

Mystics say that such knowledge comes from emptying one's heart of worldly thoughts and connecting with the Divine. This knowledge is acquired, not inherited. In Islam, God grants miracles (*muʿjizāt*, sing. *muʿjizah*) to messengers and prophets and spiritual marvels (*karāmāt*, sing. *karāmah*) to the pious people (*awli'yā*). Through this knowledge, the *awli'yā* (sing. *waliy)* sometimes may have inexplicable occurrences happen to them or see realities that are not visible to ordinary Muslims.

174. Muhammad al-Kharraz al-Baghdadi (d. 277 or 286 AH) was a famous mystic. Quoted by Al-Ghazāli in *Ihya Ulum al-Din, Kitab Sharh 'Ajā'ib al-Qalb*, translated as *The Marvels of the Heart*, trans. Walter James Skellie. (Louisville: Fons Vitae, 2010), 107.

Chapter 9

WHAT SICKENS THE HEART

"In their hearts is a disease, which Allāh has increased. A painful doom is theirs because they lie." – (Qur'ān 2:10)

The Arabs of pre-Islam, a period known as jāhiliyya, would not accompany a known liar into battle. Even though they worshiped false gods, their *fiṭrah* (innate nature) told them that a liar lacked character and integrity. Their idolatry was a much bigger lie, but they did not realize it due to their diseased hearts.

Although the above verse refers to lying as spiritual heart disease, here, it means hypocrisy. Lying and hypocrisy are the same on one level. The Pagans' saying there were gods besides God was a lie, as was their concealment of disbelief in their hearts while professing faith outwardly. But, one may ask, what does lying have to do with the heart? The answer is that, although lying is an act of the tongue, the latter only obeys the heart's command. It is a messenger, not a commander, a slave, not a master. The Meccan polytheists rejected the notion of

God's absolute authority and claimed their idols had powers alongside Him. When asked who created the heavens and earth, they said Allāh, yet they held on to their false beliefs.

While the Pagans of Mecca practiced idolatry, some of the idolaters of Medina adopted one more deadly sin: hypocrisy. Out of expediency, these Pagans professed Islam outwardly, but when they sat in the company of their fellow men, they said their allegiance was to the idols: *"And when they meet the believers, they say, 'We believe,' but when they are alone with their evil ones, they say, 'Indeed, we are with you; we were only mocking [them].'"*[175] God called both of these conditions diseases of the heart.

Ibn Taymiyah divided the heart into three types: 1) the correct heart that does not desire what goes against the commands of Allāh and His prohibitions and is free from all doubts; 2) the dead heart that neither knows its Lord nor worships Him; 3) the heart that is alive but defective. This last type contains Allāh's love, faith, and trust in Him, but it also has vain desires and low morals and manners. It continuously wavers between good and evil.[176] He called doubts and desires (*shūbūhāt* and *shahawāt*) the mother of all the heart's spiritual diseases.

Shūbūhāt

At the highest level of *shūbūhāt* is doubting God's existence, for if there is no God, then the resurrection, Judgment Day, and accountability become irrelevant. For doubters, there will

175. Qur'ān 2:14.

176. Ahmad Ibn Taymiyyah, *Diseases of the Hearts and Their Cures*, trans. Abu Rumaysah. (Birmingham, UK: Dar-us-Sunnah, 2000). The author's full name was Taqī ad-Dīn Aḥmad ibn Abd al-Halim ibn Abd al-Salam al-Numayri al-Ḥarrānī.

be no moral compass—inward or outward—to help them differentiate between right and wrong. Because their hearts become concealed in darkness, they cannot see the numerous signs that point to God's existence. The Qur'ān says: "*Behold! In the creation of the heavens and the earth, and the alternation of night and day, are indeed signs for people of understanding.*"[177] Another verse directly refers to the doubters: "*And how many signs in the heavens and the earth do they pass by? Yet they turn away from them!*"[178]

On another level, one may doubt how God will feed him and his large family. In pre-Islamic Arabia, the era of jāhilyya, some Arabs killed their children out of fear of starvation. The Qur'ān told them, "*Do not kill your children for fear of poverty, for it is We who shall provide sustenance for you as well as for them.*"[179] No one knows how many trillions of men and women God has fed since Adam and Eve. One of Satan's ploys is to whisper to people that they will become poor if they only earn by lawful means: "*Satan threatens you with poverty and orders you to commit indecency.*"[180]

A man once asked ʿAbdullāh ibn ʿAbbās, the great Qur'ānic exegete, "How does God take the souls of so many people simultaneously?" "The same way He feeds all His creations simultaneously," Ibn Abbās replied.

177. Qur'ān 3:190.

178. Qur'ān 12:105.

179. Qur'ān 6:151.

180. Qur'ān 2:268.

Shahawāt

Islam calls desires or *shahawāt* a disease of the heart because they cast a long shadow over our lives. To desire material things is not necessarily wrong, but when we want things excessively or unlawfully, we begin to live for this world and do not mind oppressing others to seize wealth, power, and fame. As a result, our hearts become inconsiderate of the needs of others. The Qur'ān offers advice on how to live and prioritize life: *"And seek the home of the Hereafter with what God has bestowed on you, [but] do not forget your portion in this world."*[181] The perfect balance lies between abandoning this world and desiring it excessively.

Once three men inquired the family of the Prophet Muhammad ﷺ about his daily worship. When informed, they decided to worship more intensely, thinking that Allāh had pardoned the Prophet's ﷺ mistakes while there was no such guarantee for them. One of them vowed to pray all night, every night, the other said he would fast every day throughout the year, and the third said he would never marry. When the Prophet ﷺ learned of their vows, he called them and said, "By Allāh, I am more conscious of Allāh than you; yet I fast and break my fast, I pray a part of the night and also sleep at night, and I marry women. So, whosoever departs from my Sunnah is not my follower."[182] The Prophet ﷺ showed them how to avoid going to extremes, even in worship.

One of the manifestations of *shahawāt* is lust. Our nature is to covet sexual pleasures, but when we pursue them without

---

181. Qur'ān 28:77.

182. Bukhārī 5063.

filters or restraints, they wreak havoc on our spirituality and family relations and damage the social fabric.

The lure of material things or lust for sexual pleasures becomes an end for some people. In their hedonism, they do not care about what is lawful and beneficial. Good life to them means they get what they want when they want it. In their Machiavellian thinking, the ends justify the means, even if the means are unlawful.

The Qur'ān equates such unbridled desires with worship: *"Have you seen him who takes his desires as his god?"*[183] When one's only goal is to fulfill their runaway desires, then no doubt these desires become their god.

When desires become god, the heart becomes devoid of spirituality. Such a heart seeks only self-gratification and pleasures. If not guarded against insatiable desires, the heart will die spiritually. The death of no other organ spells greater disaster, for the heart is the center of being, and its spiritual demise is the most significant loss anyone will ever suffer. God created our hearts and other organs to worship Him. It is not that the heart does not recognize its Creator and purpose, but our desires distract it from its goal. One way to prevent our desires from running amok is to ask if life's purpose is only to have fun or if there's a deeper meaning to life.

An American documentary[184] tells the tragic story of a family through the lens of lust gone wild. The family of four—

---

183. Qur'ān 25:43.

184. Jenny Popplewell, *American Murder: The Family Next Door,* directed by Jenny Popplewell (2020; Los Angeles: Netflix).

parents and two daughters, ages three and four—loved one another. The father doted on his adorable daughters, who extolled their dad as "my hero" in a song they sang when riding in the family van. But then tragedy struck. The father became romantically involved with another woman and eventually killed his wife, who was fifteen weeks pregnant with another child, and his two daughters. The details of the murders are too gruesome to share, but the heart-wrenching part of the murders is that when the man tried to kill his second daughter, she said, "Daddy, no!" At that point, he had already killed his wife and the other daughter. The plea of his once-beloved daughter fell on deaf ears. He killed her too, dumped his daughters' bodies in oil tanks, and buried his wife in a shallow grave nearby.

The horrific murders were an extreme manifestation of lust, for not all lust leads to murder. However, there is no doubt that lust wreaks havoc on families every year in myriad other ways.

Upon reflection, we will find that God loves us, and that's why He wants us to work on our spiritual hearts. While He allows the lowly enjoyments of this world, provided we seek them lawfully, He tells us to seek the pleasures of Paradise, which are better and everlasting.[185]

Throughout history, the wise among us aimed for the eternal prize by controlling their desires and denying themselves the excessive pleasures of this world. One way they weakened their lusts was through voluntary fasting. They understood that a

---

185. Qur'ān 87:17.

free heart means being free from the shackles of uncontrolled desires. As the following lines from a brilliant poem say,

> There is no salvation like the heart's salvation, given that
> all the limbs respond to its desires.[186]

From experience, we know that desires and doubts cause other spiritual diseases of the heart: arrogance, ostentatiousness, envy, greed, miserliness, and anger. Like Islam, in Christian theology, major diseases that destroy the heart are called the seven deadly sins: arrogance, anger, envy, laziness, greed, gluttony, and lust.

Arrogance

Arrogance was the first crime of the heart, and of all places, it happened in Paradise. Satan, who lived in Paradise amid extreme luxury and in proximity to angels and God, refused to obey God's command to bow before Adam because he considered himself better. He argued that he was superior to Adam because God created him from smokeless fire and Adam from clay. Essentially, Satan claimed racial superiority, making him the first racist.

Behind the arrogance, Satan was also envious, for he disliked the royal treatment of Adam and his wife, Eve (Ḥawwā'). Therefore, he duped them into eating from the forbidden tree to dislodge them from their privileged position

---

186. Imām al-Mawlūd's Matharat al-Qulūb, *Purification of the Heart*, trans. Hamza Yusuf. (Hayward, CA: Starlatch Press, 2004), 13.

and challenge God's decision. I will discuss the reality of Satan and his assault on humans in detail in a separate chapter.

To be arrogant or proud is to deny one's humble origins. We neither created ourselves nor the faculties on whose basis some feel superior to others. Therefore, it should be easy to conclude that pride belongs to the Creator, not the creation. Allāh said, "Pride is My cloak and greatness, My robe, and he who competes with Me in either respect I shall cast him into the Hellfire."[187]

To warn against the dangers of arrogance, the Qur'ān relates the story of rulers like Pharaoh and how God utterly destroyed them. Pharaoh, who claimed he was the great lord, had long oppressed the Children of Israel and mocked the Prophet Moses' God. God helped His prophet by parting the Red Sea for the Prophet Moses and his people and drowning Pharaoh and his army as they attempted to follow them. Pharaoh's name has become synonymous with arrogance, and, according to Islamic tradition, he will be leading his people into the Hellfire on Judgment Day.

Arrogance is the antithesis of faith, and God will forbid Paradise to the arrogant. God expelled Satan from Paradise for showing arrogance because conceit is not allowed in that hallowed place. Allāh said to Satan, *"Then get down from Paradise! It is not for you to be arrogant here. So get out! You are truly one of the disgraced."*[188]

---

187. Abī Dāwūd, Ḥadīth #4090.

188. Qur'ān 7:13.

The Prophet Muhammad ﷺ said, "No one who has a mustard seed's weight of pride in his heart shall be admitted into Paradise. And no one who has a mustard seed's weight of faith in his heart shall be admitted into the Fire." He defined arrogance as "rejecting the truth and looking down on people."

We can derive two profound rulings from the above ḥadīth. The first is that even a tiny amount of arrogance will disqualify a person from Paradise, and the second is that even an iota of faith will save a person from Hellfire. This type of disbarment from Paradise is not permanent. A person of faith with some arrogance but plenty of righteous deeds will eventually enter Paradise, but only after God purifies him of the arrogance. On the other hand, a person of weak faith, even though not cast into the Hellfire, will have to suffer some punishment for his sins before entering Paradise.

The opposite of arrogance is humility. The Prophet Muhammad ﷺ set the most remarkable example of it. He lived so nondescriptly in his community that visitors sometimes had to ask who God's messenger was. He did not have a throne or even a high chair to sit on to distinguish himself, as rulers often do. When he walked into a group of his followers, he sat wherever he could and forbade them from rising to greet him.

Humility is the way of the righteous. When the Prophet Moses and Khīḍr[189] went to a village and repaired a falling wall, the inhabitants offered no food or water to the caring strangers. The honored visitors did not complain to the locals

189. Khiḍr, according to many Muslim scholars, was a prophet, based on his story in chapter 18 of the Qur'ān. See explanation of verses 65, 66, and 82.

about their cold treatment or tell them that they enjoyed high ranks with God and that one of them was a mighty prophet.[190]

The Prophet ﷺ said that on Judgment Day, he would be "the leader of Adam's children,"[191] quickly adding that he was not saying this to show pride.

To emphasize the status of humility, the Qur'ān relates the advice of the wise man Luqmān to his son: *"And do not turn your cheek in contempt toward people and do not walk through the earth exultantly. Indeed, Allāh does not like the self-deluded and boastful."*[192]

Another verse says, *"And the servants of the Most Merciful are those who walk upon the earth with humility, and when the ignorant address them harshly, they say 'peace.'"*[193]

In a profound ḥadīth, the Prophet Muhammad ﷺ taught his Companions that all the things of this world—power, prestige, rank, and wealth—would perish one day, and it does not behoove anyone to feel pride for possessing something fleeting. So when a Bedouin's young camel beat the Prophet's ﷺ unbeaten she-camel, al-Adba, in the race, the Companions expressed sadness at al-Adba's defeat. But the Prophet ﷺ remarked: "It is Allāh's Law that He lowers or brings down whatever rises high in the world."[194] Like a Persian saying, "Every rise has a fall."

---

190. Qur'ān 18: 77, 82.

191. Muslim, Ḥadīth #2278

192. Qur'ān 31:18.

193. Qur'ān 25:63.

194. Bukhari, Ḥadīth #6501.

Through the above incident, the Prophet ﷺ also reminded his followers of what Allāh has said: *"All that is upon earth will perish, while your Lord Himself will remain forever, Possessor of Majesty and Honor."*[195]

Throughout history, mighty empires have come and gone because God alternates power among people[196] and takes it away to test who is humble in victory and patient in defeat.

'Umar ibn al-Khaṭṭāb, the second caliph, once stood in front of people in a mosque and spoke condescendingly about his humble beginnings. When his friend asked him why he did that, 'Umar said when walking into the mosque, the thought crossed his heart that he must be the best person for Muslims to have chosen him their leader, so he expelled that whisper by lowering himself in front of the people.

To keep their hearts humble, some pious people, when giving charity, put the money in their palm facing up, so the recipient's hand would be above theirs. They did not want to have the upper hand in dealing with the needy. Some even thanked the poor for accepting their charity, which they hoped would earn them God's grace.

To deter us from arrogance and remind us of how dependent we are on God, the Qur'ān tells us not to say about a thing, "I will do it tomorrow," without also saying, "if Allāh wills."[197] The rationale is that we do not know if we will even live till tomorrow, and even if we do, we might not be able to

195. Qur'ān 55:26–27.

196. Qur'ān 3:140.

197. Qur'ān 18:23–24.

do what we intended. Saying, "I will do it tomorrow," shows the certainty of power and control, which only belong to God.

We innately know that besides God, all else is perishable. The favorite poem of the sixteenth US president, Abraham Lincoln, was "Mortality" by William Knox, which begins with "O why should the spirit of mortal be proud?"[198] A sincere reflection on our origin will remind us that we are mortal, fragile, and insignificant. Allāh created Adam from clay and his progeny from a mixture of male and female fluids. Our coming into the world was a physically painful experience for our mothers. As babies, we were utterly helpless and inconsequential, a point the Qur'ān aptly reminds us of in a chapter called "The Human": "*Wasn't there a time upon man when he was not worth mentioning?* "[199]

We had no hand in our creation. Instead, someone created us and gave us all of our faculties. Then we spend the rest of our lives toiling and, upon death, return to the same earth from which God created our father, Adam.

Showing Off

One of the pillars of a pure spiritual heart is sincerity (*ikhlās*). A spiritually healthy heart is sincere to God, faith, family, and friends. God accepts good deeds only if done sincerely to earn His pleasure, not the pleasure of others. The opposite of sincerity is showing off (*ri'ya*), which also emanates from the heart. If we do a good job only to show off or to earn the praise of people, rather than for the pleasure of God, He

---

198. "William Knox," *Poets.org,* last accessed March 23, 2021, https://poets.org/poet/william-knox.

199. Qur'ān 76:1.

will not accept or reward such work. In some cases, He may punish us. God demands sincerity from us and frowns upon actions, albeit good in themselves, that we do to seek others' praise or attention.

The Qur'ān chastises Muslims who pray to show off to others.[200] Prayer, one of the most virtuous acts of worship, is rendered worthless because of flaunting, as are other righteous deeds.

The Prophet ﷺ said that a martyr, a scholar, and a wealthy philanthropist will be the first to be questioned on Judgment Day. All three will be found guilty of ostentatiousness and thrown into Hell. Allāh, Who knows what is in their hearts, will tell them they only did their noble deeds so people would praise them, which they did, so now their actions deserve punishment, not reward.[201]

In Islam, all acts of worship are praiseworthy only if done to please God. Otherwise, the doer is blameworthy. Therefore, pious Muslims check their intentions before an action: "Is this something that will please Allāh or displease Him?" The answer to "Why am I doing this?" can be found in the heart—the place of intention. The most authentic ḥadīth collection—*Ṣaḥīḥ al-Bukhārī*—begins with the prophetic saying, "Indeed actions depend on intentions, and everyone will get what he intended."[202] The ḥadīth clarifies that it is not enough to strive for good ends; the means through which we pursue them must

200. Qur'ān 107:4–6.

201. Muslim, Ḥadīth #1905.

202. Bukhārī, Ḥadīth #1.

also be lawful. In most cases, checking our hearts before doing something helps us guard against nefarious motives.

Envy

Among the things that make a heart sick is envy (*ḥasad*). Like arrogance, envy was the first crime. Satan conspired against Adam in Paradise because he was envious of Adam's high status. God created Satan before Adam from smokeless fire, supposedly the best of its kind. But then He created Adam out of clay and raised him to a higher stature. The envy moved Satan to disrespect Adam and tempt him to eat a fruit God had forbidden for him. God reprimanded Adam but forgave him when he sincerely sought forgiveness and mercy. On the other hand, Satan became defiant and blamed God for his actions. It was not enough for Satan to get Adam in trouble and cause his exit from Paradise; he swore a lasting enmity toward Adam and his progeny.

Envy was also the cause of the first murder on earth when Adam's son, Cain (*Qābīl*), killed Abel (*Hābīl*). What drove Cain to kill his brother was that God accepted Abel's sacrifice and not his because Able was pious and sincere. Both Qur'ān[203] and the Old Testament[204] tell this story.

Envy can be of two kinds. The first type is to dislike what someone else has and wish they lose it. The second type is called *ghibṭah* in Arabic, where the envier covets someone else's blessings but does not wish for him to lose them. There is no equivalent in English for *ghibṭah.*

---

203. Qur'ān 5:27.

204. Genesis 4:1–16.

Envy, with some exceptions, shows ungratefulness to God. It implies that God is unfair not to give the envier what He gave to the one envied. The Qur'ān says God bestows His favors to whomever He pleases, but He is entirely just in conferring His bounties. He alone knows what blessings are best for whom.

Interestingly, Islam allows for some *ghibṭah*, considering it good for the heart. For example, several ḥadīths say that a person may have envy, in this case, *ghibṭah,* for the wealth, knowledge, or wisdom another person has and uses to help others. But there is a fundamental difference: the envier's reason for wanting those blessings must be to use them for noble causes, like the person he envies.[205]

The story of Joseph, as told in the Qur'ān, is a classic example of envy. His half-brothers disliked that their father, Jacob, loved Joseph and Benjamin (Binyāmīn) more. Their envy reached a point where they decided to get rid of Joseph by throwing him in a deserted well. They thought that they would become the sole object of their father's love once they removed Joseph.

Envy is a form of greed, and its expulsion from the heart leads to salvation. So the Qur'ān says, *"And whosoever is saved from his greed, such are successful."*[206]

Greed

Our spiritual hearts also become sick because of greed. It's natural to covet worldly things—money, property, gold—and

205. Bukhārī, Ḥadīth #73, Muslim, Ḥadīth # 816.

206. Qur'ān 59.9.

to an extent, it's human to desire worldly things. But when our covetousness extends beyond what we need, it becomes greed, and it begins to control our lives. We are never satisfied with what we have because somebody has more than us. Greed destroys peace in our lives, and material wealth fails to make us happy. Faith departs the heart when greed occupies it.

The following ḥadīth beautifully describes our Adamic nature: "If the son of Adam had a valley full of gold, he would love to have a second one, and if he had the second one, he would love to have a third, for nothing fills the belly of Adam's son except dust."[207] The ""dust" here means death or the grave because they put a definite stop to greed.

We may not realize it, but our infatuation with buying the latest gadgets and things is a type of greed. In popular lingua, it is called consumerism. Interestingly, the term originated in Latin as "*consumere*," which means using up, eating, or wasting. It entered the English language around the medieval period and continued to carry a negative connotation. That is why at one point, the English called tuberculosis "consumption."[208] When consumerism began to get out of control, some European countries passed legislation to rein it in.

Today, consumers are not wasters. Instead, their consumerism helps the national economy. A famous saying attributed to Malcolm Forbes claims, "He who dies with the most toys wins." In a speech in the 1987 movie *Wall Street*, Gordon Gekko, played by Michael Douglas, says, "Greed, for

---

207. Bukhārī, Ḥadīth #6075; Muslim, Ḥadīth #1048.

208. "World TB Day 2020," Centers for Disease Control and Prevention, last accessed March 23, 2021, https://www.cdc.gov/tb/worldtbday/history.htm.

lack of a better word, is good." Indeed, greed is bad, and it has played havoc with economies and people's livelihoods. Several Wall Street executives have landed in jail, destroying ordinary Americans' life savings in their wake.

As said earlier, greed is part of our innate nature, and it is a test like many other kinds of desires. The Qur'ān says God has endeared to us a *"pile of gold and silver, fine branded horses, and cattle and well-tilled land, but they are only a passing enjoyment of this world, but what He has kept for the Hereafter is better and everlasting."* [209] A heart that opts for "better and everlasting" choices saves itself from the excesses of this life.

There is a story of a man who worked from early morning to late evening to accumulate wealth. He had a son who wished his father would spend some time with him. When the father came home from work one day, the son asked, "Dad, how much do you earn per hour?" When the father replied, the son gave him some dollar bills and said, "Here, can I buy one hour of your time?" The father, whose priorities were wrong but was a good-hearted person, broke into tears and promised to balance his life between work and family.

The Qur'ān strikes a perfect balance between what we need and what we want, between what is good for us and what will destroy us, and between what is short-lived and what is longer-lasting. It says, *"Seek the life of the Hereafter with what God has given you, but do not forget your rightful share in this world."*[210] In other words, live well in this world, but don't live for the world.

---

209. Qur'ān 3:14.

210. Qur'ān 28:77.

There is a big difference between eating to live and living to eat.

Miserliness

Miserliness is yet another vice that afflicts our hearts. The miser works hard to accumulate wealth but is so afraid of losing it that sometimes he does not even spend it on himself. In so doing, he becomes its first victim.

When a thief broke into the house of a man who had hoarded millions, the man pleaded with the thief, "Please kill me, but don't take my wealth because I have saved it for my old age." It didn't occur to him that if the thief were to kill him, the wealth would be of no use to him anymore.

A miser withholds money for fear of poverty. In some cases, his heart becomes so stingy that he does not even spend adequately on his children or himself. The Qur'ān tells us that the fear of poverty comes from Satan's whisper: *"Satan threatens you with poverty and orders you to immorality, while Allāh promises you forgiveness from Him and bounty. And Allāh is all-Encompassing and-Knowing."*[211]

The Prophet Muhammad ﷺ swore by his life that giving charity does not decrease one's wealth.[212] Once, he slaughtered a sheep and asked his wife, ʿĀyeshah bint Abi Bakr, to distribute its meat to the poor. When he returned home, ʿĀyeshah told him everything was "gone" except a shoulder. The Prophet ﷺ quickly corrected her, saying that what she considered "gone"

211. Qur'ān 2:268.

212. Muslim, Ḥadīth #2588.

remained with Allāh, Who will return manifold, and what she had kept, they would eat and derive only a small benefit.

If anything, charitable acts increase God's blessings and rid the heart of miserliness. Therefore, the Prophet ﷺ gave in charity even if he had to borrow. And he did so, expecting reward only from Allāh. Once, he gave away a new cloak he was wearing because someone asked for it.

The opposite of miserliness is generosity, which liberates one from the shackles of stinginess. Such a person suddenly finds himself unencumbered by the thought of poverty. The Qur'ān calls such people real winners: *"And whoso is saved from his greed, such are successful."*[213]

To insulate the heart from miserliness, the Qur'ān encourages us to spend from what we love.[214] It calls such spending the epitome of righteousness, for it is difficult to give up the best part of our wealth. Often people donate things they do not want or need anymore. They get rid of old clothes, shoes, and furniture and consider that charity. The Qur'ān says that true charity is to give something nice that we covet. Why should we give to the poor things that we would be offended if someone else were to give us?

Anger

Another disease of the heart is anger. It scorches the spiritual heart like fire destroys wood. It agitates the heart as

213. Qur'ān 64:16.

214. Qur'ān 3:92.

nothing else does. Satan looks for anger to enter the heart as a thief looks for the weakest and least-guarded point in a house.

Anger harms both the physical and spiritual hearts. For example, a Harvard Medical School study of heart attack survivors found that those who reacted angrily during conflicts were twice as likely to have another heart attack than those who handled conflict calmly.[215]

An angry person unwittingly gives momentary control over himself to Satan, who uses his victim's faculties to commit evil. One way to tell that Satan has held an angry person hostage is from the victim's remorse after his anger subsides. He is dismayed at what he did in anger. Medical science tells us that anger causes anxiety, depression, high blood pressure, heart attack, stroke, and other adverse effects.[216] It is interesting to note that anger inhibits the oxygenated blood supply to the heart and brain.

Once a man came to the Prophet Muhammad ﷺ and said, "Advise me." The Prophet ﷺ said, "Do not be angry." The man asked again, "Advise me." The Prophet ﷺ repeated his advice, "Do not be angry,"[217] three times. The advice seems simple, but we can understand its wisdom if we think deeply. How many relationships has anger ruined? How much unnecessary violence has it caused, and how remorseful has it left angry people after the anger dissipates?

---

215. M. A. Mittleman, et al., "Triggering of acute myocardial infarction onset by episodes of anger. Determinants of Myocardial Infarction Onset Study Investigators," *Circulation*, vol. 92, no. 7 (1995): 1720–1725.

216. "Anger – how it affects people," Better Health Channel, last accessed March 23, 2021, https://www.betterhealth.vic.gov.au/health/healthyliving/anger-how-it-affects-people.

217. Bukhari, Ḥadīth #5765.

Anger repulses our spiritual hearts. We do not want to be around a person who breathes fire. Anger was prevalent in the harsh desert environment of ancient Arabia. Yet, the Prophet ﷺ treated people around him exceptionally kindly, and God praises his demeanor in the following verse: *"It is by God's grace that you deal with them gently, for if you had been harsh-hearted, they would indeed have deserted you, so bear with them and pray for their forgiveness."*[218]

A ḥadīth says, "Verily, anger comes from Satan, and Satan was created from fire. Fire is extinguished with water, so if you become angry, perform ablution with water."[219] The Prophet ﷺ offered other ways of controlling anger, for example, saying, "I seek refuge in Allāh from the accursed Satan,"[220] or changing one's physical posture (sitting down if standing, or lying down if sitting).[221]

Many verses in the Qur'ān extoll the virtue of controlling anger and forgiving people. The righteous are *"Those who spend in prosperity and adversity, repress their anger, and pardon men; Verily, God loves the good-doers."*[222] The Prophet ﷺ endured tremendous abuse from his enemies, but Allāh counseled him to *"Be patient with them with what they say, then part from them graciously."*[223] The Qur'ān tells believers that when *"the ignorant people address them harshly, they should say peace"*[224] and move on.

---

218. Qur'ān 3:159.
219. Abī Dāwūd, Ḥadīth # 4784.
220. Bukhari, Ḥadīth #502.
221. Abī Dāwūd, Ḥadīth #4764.
222. Qur'ān 3:134.
223. Qur'ān 73:10.
224. Qur'ān 25:63.

Not all anger is blameworthy, though. It is virtuous to be angry against tyranny and injustice. If people did not use their anger to push back on crimes and oppression, criminals would commit their dastardly deeds with impunity, and society would be doomed. One reason why so much injustice exists today is that people, in general, have not shown what we may call righteous anger against it. A ḥadīth says that we should fight evil with our hands; if we cannot do that, then with our speech; if we cannot do that, we should hate it in our hearts. Fighting in the heart means having disgust for evil. Taking a stand against evil involves different degrees of resolve and anger, and we know not everyone is capable of using their hands or speaking out due to the fear of retribution.

The Prophet ﷺ himself became angry when he saw people mocking or violating God's laws. The Companions could tell it from his face, which generally carried a smile. But he never used foul language or screamed in anger. So, being angry can be praiseworthy in the proper context. All God's prophets showed anger at times, but they controlled it instead of letting it control them. For example, the Prophet Moses used his fist to strike a man who was oppressing one of his people. He also became furious when he learned that his people had begun worshiping a golden calf when he went to Mount Sinai. He threw down the Ten Commandments and angrily accosted his brother Aaron (Hārūn), asking why he had let that happen in his absence.

When 'Umar ibn al-Khaṭṭāb became Muslim, he used his anger to defend and protect Islam, and the Prophet ﷺ did not chastise him for it.

Last but not least, practicing to smile frequently can help tame anger. The Prophet ﷺ smiled frequently. Indeed, his followers considered him the most smiling person in the community. He even advised others to smile when meeting someone, calling a smile a small charity.

Dr. Earlexia Norwood, a family medicine practitioner in Troy, Michigan, says, "Smiling is contagious, and when we smile, we activate neurons in the brain that fire a synchronizing feature. You'll notice that one smile will lead to additional smiles, not just for you, but [also] for those around you."[225]

Applying the benefit of a smile to the heart, we can say through experience that a smiling person's heart feels tranquil and not agitated, as an angry person's heart does.

---

225. Earlexia Norwood, "Surprising Health Benefits of Smiling," http://www.henryfordlivewell.com/health-benefits-smiling.

Chapter 10

THE BLIGHT OF SINS

"Corruption has appeared on land and sea because of the evil which men's hands have done: and so that He will make them taste the consequences of some of their doings, perhaps that they may turn back from evil." – (Qur'ān 30:41)

Sins don't just afflict the heart. They also corrupt what the heart touches. We can call the latter the heart's "collateral" victims. The above verse reminds us of brutal dictators, war-ravaged countries and refugees, polluted seas, the smog of cities, melting glaciers, California bushfires, and acid rain, to name a few. Although the verse calls "men's hands" the culprit, it is the heart that commands the limbs to do its bidding. Men with corrupt hearts have shown us what evil they can perpetrate on the world.

Sin's first victim is the heart itself. The Prophet Muhammad ﷺ said, "Verily when the servant sins, a dark mark appears upon his heart. His heart will be polished if he abandons the sin, seeks forgiveness, and repents. If he returns to the sin, the darkness will increase until it overcomes his heart."[226] The Prophet then recited this verse of the Qur'ān: "*No! Their deeds have cast a veil over their hearts.*"[227]

The dark covering on the heart prevents it from seeing the light of faith. Such a heart cannot receive light from outside, nor can it emit light from inside, if it has any. Such a heart cannot tell right from wrong. In essence, such a heart fails to see the path of salvation or realize the purpose behind its creation. When a heart reflects on the wondrous signs within the Qur'ān, it can discern the truth; otherwise, it is like a locked-up heart that cannot see beyond its narrow confines. The Qur'ān draws profound imagery of an unreflecting heart: "*Do they not then reflect on the Qur'ān? Or are there locks upon their hearts?*"[228]

There are reports that when some Muslim scholars forgot a verse during recitation in prayer, they attributed it to a sin they may have committed. Similarly, others said that an act of their disobedience to Allāh caused them to be lazy in optional nightly prayer (*tahajjud*).

Imam Abu Hanīfah, the famous exegete, once accidentally stepped on the foot of a child in the street, upon which the latter cried, "Don't you fear Allāh?" The scholar began to shake and would have fallen if his friend had not propped him. "O Imam, why are you so shaken? It's just a child!" the friend said. Abu Hanīfah responded, "And how would I know if Allāh is not warning me through this child?" That was the

226. Tirmidhi, Ḥadīth #3334.

227. Qur'ān 83:14.

228. Qur'ān 47:24.

level of faith in the pious. A minor incident would fill their hearts with self-reproach and make them worried if they had displeased their Lord.

When the stone throwers of Ṭā'if bloodied the Prophet Muhammad ﷺ in response to his calling them to Islam, he did not care about himself but instead wondered whether it happened because he had somehow displeased Allāh. His soulful supplication should resonate with all those facing difficulties and wondering if Allāh is displeased with them.

> O Allāh, to You, do I complain of the weakening of my strength, of my few options, of the way people humiliate me; O Most Merciful of the merciful ones, You are the Lord of the weak ones, and You are my Lord. To whom will You entrust me? To a distant (stranger) who will show me an unwelcome face or an enemy, whom You have given control over my situation? If You are not angry with me, then I do not care. I seek refuge with the light of Your Face, which removes darkness and sets the affairs of the world and the Hereafter aright, that Your anger descends upon me, or Your displeasure befall me. I will continue to seek Your pleasure until You become pleased (with me). And there is neither might nor power except with You.[229]

One of the lessons the Prophet's ﷺ prayer teaches us is introspection. He did not curse the stone throwers or rejectors but looked inward for the fault that might have brought

229. Muhammad Ibn Ishāq, Sirāt Rasūl Allāh, *The Life of Muhammad*, 27th ed., trans. A. Guillaume. (Karachi: Oxford University Press, 2014), 193. The quote has been slightly modified. Various Seerah books have recorded this supplication with somewhat different wordings.

the rejection and attack upon him. When hearts humble themselves, Allāh elevates them. Such hearts go through two competing emotions. They fear that their sins will anger their Lord and hope that He will be merciful. Allāh praises the Prophet Zechariah (Zakariyya) and his wife in the Qur'ān for embodying these two traits: *"They used to hasten to do good, and call on Us in hope and fear and were always humble before Us."*[230]

Some hearts become hard as stone, even harder. As mentioned earlier, even stones split or hollow out to make way for a waterfall. But some men have hearts of steel that show no mercy. A man saw the Prophet Muhammad ﷺ kissing his grandchildren and remarked proudly, "I have ten children, and I do not kiss any of them." The Prophet ﷺ said, "Verily, whoever does not show mercy will not receive mercy,"[231] meaning God's mercy. Whatever mercy we show to others is a tiny fraction of our Creator's mercy that He bestowed on us.

There is a connection between our mercy toward others and God's mercy toward us. The Prophet ﷺ told his followers that if they showed mercy to those on earth, the One Who is in the heavens will reciprocate with the same.[232] No doubt, God's mercy is far superior. An Arabic adage says, *kamā tūdīnū tūdān*, as you treat others, others will treat you. It is similar to what Abu ad-Dardā, a Companion of the Prophet ﷺ, said, "Be as you will, for as you judge, you shall be judged,"[233] or the

230. Qur'ān 21:90.

231. Bukhārī, Ḥadīth #5651, Muslim, Ḥadīth #2318.

232. Tirmidhī, Ḥadīth #1924.

233. This is an athar, a statement of the Companion of the Prophet Muhammad, quoted from Zuhd of Aḥmad ibn Ḥanbal, quote #448.

"golden rule" of life: "Do unto others what you want others to do unto you."

One of the harms of sin is that it makes the heart heedless. The first sin usually bothers a person, but the one-hundredth sin hardly makes a ripple in his heart. The frequency of sins makes them appear insignificant in his eyes, and he does not care anymore if people know about them. The Qur'ān describes what happens next:

"Have you seen the one who has taken his desires as his god? And so Allāh, out of knowledge, left him astray, sealed his hearing and heart, and placed a cover on his sight. Who then can guide him after Allāh? Will you then not take heed?"[234]

Indeed, in the worst case, such a person's heart becomes so corroded that he displays his sins proudly as one displays medals. Alas, how many businesses glorify their products, which corrupt the heart! From alcohol to cigarettes to pornography, these industries' effects are catastrophic on society. They use deception for marketing their harmful products. A cigarette ad shows smiling young men and women with the caption, "Alive with Pleasure," even though the package displays a warning in bold letters from the US surgeon-general that smoking kills.

According to the National Institutes of Health, 95,000 Americans die annually from alcohol-related causes. The financial loss is upwards of $250 billion and contributes to more than 200 diseases and injuries, including liver cirrhosis and cancers. A staggering "more than 10 percent of US

234. Qur'ān 45:23.

children live with a parent with alcohol problems, according to a 2012 study."[235]

Smoking causes far greater devastation. The Centers for Disease Control says that 480,000 Americans die per year in the United States from smoking, including more than 41,000 deaths from secondhand smoke exposure. It makes smoking the leading cause of preventable death in the US. The economic cost is over $300 billion annually.[236] Despite the colossal damage smoking wreaks, the tobacco industry spends billions of dollars each year on advertising to sell its products with governmental acquiescence.

More than 500 studies on the effects of pornography have concluded that it is harmful to all age groups. It desensitizes the viewer. It is addictive, degrades marriages, and encourages other crimes.[237] Another set of studies calls it a "public health crisis." It is a social and physical toxin that destroys relationships, steals innocence, erodes compassion, breeds violence, and kills love."[238] Interestingly, the word "pornography" comes from the Greek words "porne" (prostitute) and "graphos" (to write/record). So it literally means "recorded prostitution."

The Qur'ān calls such sins *al-faḥshā* (indecency), and they happen because the sinner has allowed an easy pass to Satan

---

235. "Alcohol Abuse in the United States," National Institute on Alcohol Abuse and Alcoholism, last accessed March 23, 2021, www.niaaa.nih.gov/publications/brochures-and-fact-sheets/alcohol-facts-and-statistics.

236. "Smoking & Tobacco Use," Centers for Disease Control and Prevention, last accessed March 23, 2021, www.cdc.gov/tobacco/data_statistics/fact_sheets/fast_facts/index.htm#beginning.

237. American Life League, "The Harmful Effects of Pornography," EWTN.com, last accessed March 23, 2021, https://www.ewtn.com/catholicism/library/harmful-effects-of-pornography-9664.

238. "Porn Harms," Endsexualexploitation.org, last accessed March 23, 2021, https://endsexualexploitation.org/pornography/.

and the lower self. If one reflects on the nature of pornography, it becomes evident that it is degrading and dehumanizing. Many of those who act in pornographic movies are victims of sex-trafficking gangs. And those who view pornography suffer from a loss of love, respect, and compassion for their spouses. Some even resort to sexual crimes or violence to satiate their desires. All of them experience a loss of self-esteem.

The Qur'ān says, *"Do not go near adultery. It is truly a shameful deed and an evil way."* [239] The command shows God's perfect wisdom. Adultery is an abomination, so He forbids anything that could lead to it. Many sinful ideas enter a person's heart through the eyes; therefore, turning away from looking at shameful things will avert the harm.

Muhammad ibn Ismāʿīl al-Bukhārī, the compiler of the most authentic ḥadīth collection, has an entire chapter called "*Kitāb al-Riqāq*" (Book of Softening of the Hearts), as do some of the other ḥadīth scholars. In this chapter, the many prophetic sayings dwell on this world's transience and contrast it with the Hereafter's eternality and superiority. Upon close examination, one can discern the wisdom behind these reminders. If people remember that this world is temporary and the Day of Reckoning is near, they will guard their hearts against too much love for this world. They will not be whom the Qur'ān warns: *"The greed for more has distracted you [from God] until you ended up in the grave."* [240]

239. Qur'ān 17:32.

240. Qur'ān 102:1–2.

Indeed, the unfettered pursuit of wealth seems delusional because death suddenly cuts us off from it. The much-vaunted riches become our children's inheritance, over which they might fight and spend recklessly. Does it not beg reflection that the shroud in which people bury their dead has no pockets? It does not need to.

The preponderance of unrepented sin pushes sinners away from Allāh and darkens their spiritual hearts. It may be alive outwardly but gravely ill or even dead spiritually. Allāh warns against the consequences of abandoning Him because it will cause the heart to forget its purpose and wander in misguidance.

The Qur'ān says that "*God is the light of the heavens and the earth.*" [241] He is also the One Who illuminates our hearts and fuels the flame of faith within them. The closer we are to God, the brighter our hearts shine. Nearness to God signifies a higher status with Him, the same way as in a king's court, the most elevated in rank sit closest to the king.

The worst consequence of forgetting Allāh will be that He will "forget" such a person on Judgment Day: "*This Day We shall forget you, as you forgot your meeting of this Day.*" [242] It is not for God to forget anything; the verse implies that on Judgment Day, God will veil from His mercy those who died as a disbeliever. This case is different from a sinner who believes in God and the Hereafter and can hope for God's mercy.

---

241. Qur'ān 24:35.

242. Qur'ān 45:34.

A direct result of sin is God's indifference to our supplications. God hears all supplications but does not grant every one of them. The Prophet ﷺ said, Allāh is good (*al-Ṭayyab*) and accepts only good. Then he described a person who stretches out his hand in supplication but whose food, drink, and clothes are from unlawful income. "Then how can his supplication be accepted?"[243] God rejects a supplication that does not meet His criteria like a court declines a petition that violates its laws. In Islam, God grants those prayers that seek positive things but not those that ask for forbidden things or cut off kinship ties.

Another effect of sin is that it pushes the sinner's heart into despair. A hopeless person might say, "What's the point in doing any good anymore?" Satan whispers this excuse to a persistent sinner to keep him from repenting and reforming. "If there is no hope for redemption," Satan suggests to the sinner, "you might as well continue to enjoy life." Satan knows that to lose hope in God's mercy is a greater sin than any a person might have committed. The merciful God looks for sincere repentance and future abstinence from sin to forgive a person, but Satan does not want his victim to know this.

Sin darkens the spiritual heart while knowledge illuminates it. They reside in the same heart but to the exclusion of each other. Knowledge retreats when sins overtake the heart, leaving the heart in darkness. It is a great loss because we become God-conscious and know our life's purpose through knowledge. Without the *gnosis* of God, our hearts lose direction.

---

243. Muslim, the Book of Zakāt, Ḥadīth #1015.

Sins displease Allāh, and that is no ordinary matter. The repercussions of sin go beyond this world. The Prophet ﷺ said, "When Allāh is angry with a servant, He calls Gabriel and says: 'I dislike this person, so you should dislike him.' Then Gabriel dislikes him and announces in the heavens: 'Verily, Allāh dislikes this person, so you should dislike him.' Thus, the heavens' inhabitants dislike him, and he is hated on the earth."[244]

The Qur'ān sternly warns: *"But whoever turns away from My Reminder will undoubtedly have a miserable life, then We will raise him blind on the Day of Judgment, and he will ask, 'My Lord! Why have you raised me blind when I used to see before?' Allāh will respond, "It is because Our revelations came to you and you neglected them, so on this Day will you be neglected.'"*[245]

Among sin's effects is that it leads to more sins. A cheater lies to conceal his crime. A drunkard may murder or rape under intoxication. Some drug addicts might rob others to support their addiction. The Prophet ﷺ admonished, "Beware of lying as lying leads to transgression and transgression leads to the Fire."[246] We see that sin has a cascading effect.

Sins lead to a person losing God's esteem for him. Although the merciful God likes all His creations, He does not like their sinful deeds. Some people suggest that God should love them all in all circumstances, whether they are good or evil. That defies wisdom. It would be unfair to a homicide victim if a judge loved his murderer. God has guidelines for bringing

---

244. Bukhārī, Ḥadīth #3037, Muslim, Ḥadīth #2637.

245. Qur'ān 20:124–126.

246. Muslim, Ḥadīth #2607.

people closer to Him and what distances them from Him. Some actions endear us to God, and others invoke His wrath. Scattered throughout the Qur'ān are verses that inform readers about actions God does not like. Many verses tell us what God does like: righteousness and justice, kindness and truthfulness, and forgiveness and good manners. Here, however, we will discuss things that God dislikes.

Some of the people God does not like are:

- the rejectors of faith (3:32),
- the ungrateful (2:276), and the sinful,
- the corruption mongers (5:64),
- the transgressors (2:190),
- the oppressors (3:140),
- the treacherous sinners (4:107),
- the embezzlers (8:58),
- the proud and boastful (4:36),
- the arrogant (16:23), and
- the extravagant (7:31)

Space does not allow us to dwell on all categories.

Ibn Al Qayyim Al-Jawzīyyah points out that sins bring destruction upon the sinners. For example, Satan got kicked out of Paradise because of the sin of arrogance. Other actors or nations that God destroyed due to sins were Pharaoh and

Korah (Qārūn) and the nations of Prophets Noah, Eber (Hūd), and Shelah (Ṣāleḥ).[247]

The Prophet ﷺ warned that "When evil appears on the earth, Allāh sends down his punishment upon its inhabitants."[248] The ḥadīth echoes what the Qur'ān says, *"And whatever of misfortune befalls you, it is because of what your own hands have earned."*[249]

In the age of heightened individualism, people think of their sins as an expression of personal freedom, not realizing that what they do can and does affect society. That is why societies have laws regulating what people can and cannot do. A ḥadīth tells the example of passengers on the lower deck of a ship telling those on the upper deck that they will make a hole in the bottom, but those on the upper deck should not worry about it. If the upper deck were to allow it, everyone would drown.[250] It affects everyone, whether loggers recklessly mow down Amazon forests or factories callously dump chemical waste in the ocean or their chimneys spew toxic smoke into the sky.

In Islam, at least a group of people must enjoin good and forbid evil (*amr bi'l mā'rūf nahī 'ani'l mūnkar*). Otherwise, God will punish everyone, even those complicit through their silence: *"Beware of a trial that will not only affect the wrongdoers among you."*[251]

---

247. Imam Ibnul Qayyim Al-Jawziyyah, *Spiritual Disease and Its Cure.* (London: Darussalam), 58–59.

248. Al-Mu'jam al-Awsaṭ, Ḥadīth # 2110.

249. Qur'ān 42:30.

250. Bukhārī, Ḥadīth #2361.

251. Qur'ān 8:25.

Chapter 11

THE HEART'S WEAPON

"Supplication is a believer's weapon."[252] – (Ḥadīth)

The above ḥadīth tells us that supplication (*du'ā*) is a weapon against the heart's decay, Satan's mischiefs, and the lower self's avarice. Supplication is like a shield that protects its owner against attack. *Du'ā* in Arabic can mean several things, including an invitation, a prayer, or a call, but here we shall use this term primarily to describe supplicating or praying to Allāh and how it comforts our hearts.

The heart is the bifunctional and most crucial organ in our body. Our physical survival depends on the heart continuing to beat in our chests, and our spiritual survival relies on faith residing within the heart. However, faith (*īmān*) cannot flourish without righteous actions (*'amal ṣāleḥ)*. That's why the Qur'ān describes the successful as those who have *īmān* and do *amal ṣāleh* together. We must also add supplication as another

252. "Musnad Abu Ya'la," Ḥadīth #439.

indispensable component for the spiritual heart's success. Supplication to God is a sign of faith and is a righteous action of the heart.

A person manifests disbelief by not asking Allāh to guide his heart and forgive his sins. Allāh says, *"Call upon Me; I will respond to you. Surely those too arrogant to worship Me will enter Hell, disgraced."*[253] Here, "worship" means supplication because the Prophet ﷺ said, "Supplication *is* worship."[254]

The supplication that the Prophet Muhammad ﷺ said most often was to ask Allāh to strengthen his heart.[255] The Prophet's ﷺ heart already overflowed with righteousness, yet he understood that the way to keep it steady was through continued good actions and supplication to Allāh. In *Sūrah* Āal Imrān, the Qur'ān describes the "people of understanding" as those who remain concerned that faith might depart from their hearts. Thus, they pray, *"Our Lord, let not our hearts deviate after You have guided us and grant us Your mercy. Indeed, You are the Bestower."*[256] These people jealously guard their faith and do not take it for granted. They do everything to preserve it in their hearts and manifest it through their actions, knowing faith can weaken. As an added measure of security, they ask the One Who bestowed faith in the first place to preserve it in their hearts forever.

Du'ā was the heart and soul of every prophet of God. Day in and day out, they invoked their Lord for blessings and forgiveness and sought His help against calamities. Those

---

253. Qur'ān 40:60.

254. Tirmidhī Ḥadīth #3247.

255. Tirmidhī, Ḥadīth #2140.

256. Qur'ān 3:8.

supplications are too many to include in this book, but here are a few.

The Prophet Adam, when he and his wife erred into eating from the forbidden tree, sought Allāh's forgiveness from the depths of their hearts: *"Our Lord, we have wronged ourselves, and if You do not forgive us and have mercy upon us, we will surely be among the losers."*[257] The Prophet Abraham asked God to show him how He gives life to the dead. When God asked, *"Do you not believe?"* he replied, *"Yes, I do, but for the reassurance of my heart."*[258] The Prophet Jonah (Yūnūs) called out for forgiveness from inside the whale's belly. He was angry with his people and left them without God's permission. Then he boarded a ship to flee, but the captain threw him overboard to save the overladen vessel. A whale promptly swallowed him. The Prophet Jonah said this heartfelt prayer as a prisoner in the whale's belly: "*There is no god except You. Glory be to You! I have certainly done wrong.*" [259] In his prayer, the Prophet Jesus asked God to show mercy toward the sinners,[260] and the Prophet Muhammad ﷺ implored: "O God, I seek refuge with You from the knowledge not beneficial, from a heart not humble, from a soul not satisfied, and from a supplication not answered."[261]

The supplication to God protects the heart from becoming arrogant. It reminds us that our deeds are not a guarantor of success but only a means. We only need to look at our failed efforts to understand this. A farmer sows the seed and waters

---

257. Qur'ān 7:23.

258. Qur'ān 2:260.

259. Qur'ān 21:87.

260. Qur'ān 5:118.

261. Nasā'ī, Ḥadīth #5537.

it, but it is not up to him to make the seed sprout. Every farmer knows this from botched crops. When the farmer asks God to make the seed sprout, he has sought someone Who *can* make this happen.

For a righteous deed to achieve real success, it must receive God's acceptance because that is the crowning moment of our good works. Believers, therefore, pray to God to accept their efforts. When the Prophet Abraham was raising the foundations of the *Kaʿbah* with his elder son, Ishmael (Ismāʿīl), for the worship of One God, he knew his actions needed acceptance from on high, and so he prayed: "*Our Lord, accept this from us. Indeed You are the Hearing, the Knowing.*"[262] God accepted his prayers and made the *Kaʿbah* a center of worship.

Supplicating for Others

In Islam, one may also pray for others. Doing so is a noble act. It pleases God that one has concern for the well-being of others. A ḥadīth says that "Whenever a Muslim supplicates for his brother-in-faith in his absence, the angels say: 'May the same be for you too.'"[263] It would touch our hearts deeply to find out that someone prayed for us in absentia. People sometimes backbite others, a practice Islam calls *ghībah* and categorizes as a major sin. Wishing someone well or speaking highly of them behind their backs is the opposite of *ghībah* and shows sincerity. A prayer said for someone in their absence shows genuine love. By such a prayer, the doer does not seek

262. Qur'ān 2:127.

263. Riyād as-Sālīhīn, Ḥadīth #1494.

to impress the subject or earn the person's favor but genuinely wishes the person well.

Across other religious and cultural traditions, we find people wishing others "good luck," "good morning," and "have a blessed day." People in difficulty often ask others—a neighbor, a friend, even a stranger—to "pray for me." The belief that prayer benefits us is ingrained in our hearts. Sometimes, nonbelievers subconsciously cry out to the Divine during a tragedy: "God, please help me!" After a complicated surgery, a doctor may say, "Pray, now it is in God's hands." It's also interesting that people will instinctively say "Oh my God," when surprised by something or "Thank God" after escaping a disaster.

While we must pray to God for ourselves, the prayers of the pious on our behalf have a higher status and are more readily accepted. Allāh commanded the Prophet Muhammad ﷺ to pray for the sinners in his community: *"And pray for them—indeed your prayer is a source of comfort for them. And Allāh is All-Hearing, All-Knowing. Do they not know that Allāh accepts the repentance of His servants and their charity and that Allāh alone is the Acceptor of Repentance, Most Merciful?"* [264] The Prophet ﷺ regularly prayed for all people, even those who attacked him. He feared God's retribution against those who abused him and pleaded: "My Lord, forgive my people for they do not know."[265] In Luke 23:34, Prophet Jesus makes a similar supplication, calling upon Allāh to "forgive them, for they do not know what they are doing." When someone suggested to the Prophet Muhammad

264. Qur'ān 9:103–104.

265. Bukhārī, Hadith #6530.

ﷺ that he invoke God's wrath against a hostile tribe, he instead prayed, "O Allāh, guide them."

Once a Bedouin prayed, "O Allāh! Bestow Your mercy on Muhammad ﷺ and me only, and do not bestow it on anybody else." The Prophet ﷺ told him, "You have restricted a very vast thing,"[266] meaning Allāh's mercy. The lesson from this incident is that God's mercy, bounty, and generosity are boundless, and seeking good for others does not diminish our own rewards. On the contrary, praying for the well-being of others and others doing the same for us makes our hearts feel good.

Supplication impacts every facet of life. The more we supplicate, the more assured our hearts feel. Allāh not only asks us to call upon Him, but He has also allowed us to ask others to supplicate for us. The theological term for asking others is *tawassul* or intermediation. One may ask a pious person to pray for him, given the latter's presumed proximity to God. Most Muslim scholars say *tawassul* may not be sought from a dead person, no matter how pious. The Prophet's ﷺ Companions regularly asked him to pray for them while he was alive. Muslims believe that on Judgment Day, the Prophet Muhammad ﷺ will supplicate for all humanity.

Du'ā Repels Predestiny

The Prophet ﷺ said, "Nothing repels Allāh's predestiny except *du'ā*."[267] This ḥadīth teaches us that a sincere supplication can avert a misfortune that God had decreed for

---

266. Bukhārī, Vol 8, Book 73, Hadith #39.

267. Tīrmīdhī, Ḥadīth #139, Ibn Mājah, Ḥadīth #90.

a person. Another rule we derive is that we should not resign to our difficulties but instead act to change them. Prayer is one form of action that can repel predestiny (*qadr*).

According to the famous tradition called Ḥadīth Jibrīl,[268] Allāh has predestined good and evil for us. The ups and downs of our lives are part of predestiny, as are our actions. For example, a person may get sick, but due to his supplication, Allāh cures him, as happened to the Prophet Job (Ayyūb). He lost his children in a calamity and suffered through a prolonged, painful disease. After nearly two decades of suffering, he called out to Allāh for help. The help came: *"So We responded to him and removed the harm that afflicted him. And We gave him back his family and more like them, as a mercy from Us and a reminder for the worshippers."*[269]

According to sound scholarly opinion, *du'ā* can change the intermediate *qadr* but not the final *qadr*. Due to the Prophet's ﷺ supplication, 'Umar ibn al-Khaṭṭāb accepted Islam; however, Abu Jahl and two of the Prophet's ﷺ uncles did not. Ibn al-Qayyim said that supplication could permanently repel a predestiny if stronger than it, soften it if weaker, or block it if of the same strength.[270]

Supplication is God's remembrance, which in turn makes the heart tranquil. It is an admission of our helplessness and humility before God's power and majesty. The more a

---

268. Muslim, Ḥadīth #8.

269. Qur'ān 21:84.

270. Al-Dā' wa al-Dawā', *The Illness and Medicine*. (al-Mansoura, Egypt: Dar Al-Manarah, 2010), 42. See also Yasir Qadhi, Du'ā, *The Weapon of the Believer*. (Birmingham, UK: Al-Hidaayah Publishing and Distribution Ltd, 2003), 51.

slave praises his master, the more the master gives. If this is generally the situation with the masters of this world, we can only imagine what the Master of the Universe can give from His inexhaustible treasures and generosity.

A Prayer for Every Occasion

Supplication covers every aspect of a Muslim's life, literally from the cradle to the grave. Muslims begin and end the day with God's glorification. There is a prayer for husband-and-wife intimacy, conception, the birth of righteous children, a good end to this life, ease in the grave, and admission into Paradise. There are also prayers related to eating, traveling, rain, lunar and solar eclipses, knowledge, wealth, and cures.

The Prophet ﷺ taught his Companions supplications for different occasions, including before a battle, during the last third of the night, during the ritual prayer, while performing 'Umrah and Ḥajj, visiting the sick, or a cemetery.

Some prayers are specific and limited in scope, like asking Allāh to help win a competition, while others are comprehensive and overarching, like *"My Lord, increase me in knowledge,"*[271] or *"Our Lord, grant us the good of this world and the good of the Hereafter, and save us from Hellfire."*[272]

The Prophet ﷺ and his Companions asked Allāh for guidance in every matter, even the most mundane ones. Therefore, one of the prayers in Islam is *Ṣalāt al-Istīikhārah,* the Prayer of Seeking Counsel. Before making an important life

---

271. Qur'ān 20:114.

272. Qur'ān 2:201.

decision, a person offers two prayer units and asks God which way to proceed.

The Prophet ﷺ said,

> When one of you has a concern, let him perform two prayer cycles besides the obligatory prayers. Then, let him say, "O Allāh, I seek guidance from your knowledge and power from your might, and I ask you for your tremendous favor. Verily, you have power, and I do not, and you know, and I do not. You are the Knower of the unseen. O Allāh, if you know this matter to be good for my religion, livelihood, and end, or if it is better for my present and later needs, decree it for me and make it easy for me and bless me in it. But if you know this matter to be evil for my religion, livelihood, and end, or if it is worse for my present and later needs, then divert it from me and keep me away from it, and decree what is good for me and then make me content with it." Then mention his need.[273]

Any decision about the future involves the unseen. Since none of us knows the future, asking God from His infinite knowledge of the future seems like a logical and wise choice. Even the Prophet ﷺ, divinely guided as he was, did not know the future except by Allāh's leave. Allāh told him to tell his detractors, *"If I knew the unseen, I would have benefited myself enormously, and no harm would have ever touched me. I am only a warner and deliverer of good news for those who believe."*[274] Have all of us not

273. Bukhārī, Ḥadīth #1113.

274. Qur'ān 7:188.

run into situations when a job we happily took turned out to be a big disappointment or a decision we made with excitement backfired? How often have we felt sad about a lost opportunity, only to find out the ugly truth and say, "Thank God I didn't get it!" The Qur'ān says, *"It may be that you hate a thing and it is good for you, and it may be that you love a thing and it is bad for you. And Allāh knows while you know not."*[275]

While the Qur'ān and the Prophet's ﷺ Sunnah teach the best supplications, a person is free to supplicate in their own words and language. Therefore, although the Creator knows our needs, He wants us to verbalize our prayers.

Supplications are a way of reaching the goal, which means we must make the effort to reach that goal and not think that supplication alone can take care of our needs. For example, when a camel rider asked the Prophet Muhammad ﷺ, "O Messenger of Allāh, should I tie my camel and trust Allāh, or should I leave her untied and trust Allāh," the Prophet ﷺ replied, "Tie her and trust Allāh."[276] Trusting Allāh (*tawakkūl*) does not mean negating the necessity of one's efforts; it necessitates it. The same applies to supplication, which one must support through other means. The man's camel could have wandered off had he not tied her, but the Prophet ﷺ taught him the correct method of relying on Allāh.

Ways to Supplication

Just as a weapon is most effective when used correctly, a supplication is most useful when done right. Therefore, God

275. Qur'ān 2:116.

276. Tirmīdhī, Ḥadīth #2517.

urges us to supplicate to Him for all our needs. However, one may ask a fellow human for something, knowing the ultimate giver is the One Who owns our lives and all else. Two of Allāh's names are *al-Wahhāb*, the Bestower, and *Dhi al-Ṭhawl*, the Owner of Abundance. So, whatever someone gives us is from what God gave them.

Although God is always eager to grant our prayers, we must not ask Him for something unlawful. God is *good,* and He only grants *good* prayers. Therefore, one of the quintessential prayer requirements is sincerity and conviction in the heart that God will accept it. The Prophet ﷺ said, "Call upon Allāh with certainty that He will answer you. Know that Allāh will not answer the supplication of an unmindful and distracted heart."[277]

Like all things, supplication has its etiquette. We should start our supplication by praising Allāh by His majestic names, such as the Forgiving, the Generous, the High, the Almighty, and the Grantor of Prayer. We should thank Him for the favors He has already granted. We should also invoke His blessings upon the Prophet ﷺ before presenting our request.

Prayer is a positive experience and must not be tainted with negative thoughts about others. A supplicator may not ask for someone's destruction or removal of Allāh's bounty upon him unless it is against a tyrant and evil person. Even in that case, we are encouraged first to ask God to guide them. We should not be hasty and complain about why God has not accepted

277. Tīrmīdhī, Ḥadīth #3479.

our prayer yet because that would make us abandon our supplication.

A believer should know that God accepts all good prayers but in His way and at the time He knows is best for us. Sometimes, God may use the supplicator's prayer to elevate their rank in the Hereafter instead of giving what they asked of this world or expiate a sin. Giving a person something other than what they asked for can manifest God's mercy. Sometimes what we ask for can get us in trouble. For example, a mother would never give her toddler red-hot coal to play with out of mercy, no matter how hard he cries. So what then about the merciful God!

Although God gives day and night, there are times and places where He is more accepting of supplications, such as the last third of the night, in the Night of Decree (*Laylat ul-Qadr*),[278] and inside the Kaʿbah and other blessed places. When the Prophet Zechariah visited Mary in the secluded area of the house of worship, he would find beside her out of season fruits. It appeared to be a miracle. When he asked Mary about the fruits, she said they came from Allāh. Some say that the Prophet Zechariah considered the niche (*mīhrāb*) where the fruits lay to be a hallowed place, and that is why he immediately raised his hands in prayer: *"My Lord! Grant me—by your grace—righteous offspring. You are certainly the Hearer of prayers. So the angels called out to him while he stood praying in the mīhrāb, 'Allāh gives you good news of the birth of Yaḥyā (John the Baptist) who will confirm the*

278. *Laylat ul-Qadr* occurs on one of the last five odd nights of Ramadan.

Word of Allāh and will be a great leader, chaste, and a prophet among the righteous.'"[279]

The preferred times for supplications are Fridays, the first ten days of *Dhul Ḥijjah*, during rain, and while traveling. In addition, some supplications have a higher priority with God, such as a father's prayer for his children, an oppressed person's prayer, that of a just ruler, and a fasting person's invocation as they break their fast.

Supplications are not limited to humans. Even angels pray. The Qur'ān refers to the angels' prayer for believers:

> *Our Lord! You encompass everything in Your mercy and knowledge. So forgive those who repent and follow Your Way, and protect them from the torment of the Hellfire. Our Lord! Admit them into the Gardens of Eternity You have promised them and the righteous among their parents, spouses, and descendants. You are indeed the Almighty, All-Wise. Protect them from the consequences of their evil deeds, for whoever You protect from the evil of their deeds on that Day will have been shown Your mercy. That is truly the ultimate triumph.*[280]

Finally, supplications are not just weapons or shields of protection against this world's troubles and the torment of the Hellfire; they are also a means of asking God to bless us with a good heart, righteous children, actions that please Him, and Paradise.

279. Qur'ān 3:38–39.

280. Qur'ān 40:7–9.

The Prophets' Prayers

God's prophets supplicated at all hours of the day and night. Their supplications were exuberant and hopeful. Here I quote a small sampling.

Adam: *"Our Lord! We have wronged ourselves. If You forgive us not, and bestow not upon us Your Mercy, we shall certainly be of the losers."* (Qur'ān 7:23). It is the first-ever supplication, and it took place in Paradise.

Jonah): *"None has the right to be worshiped, but You, Glorified and Exalted are You. Indeed, I have been of the wrong-doers."* (Qur'ān 21:87). He said this prayer in the belly of the whale. The Prophet Muhammad ﷺ said, "A Muslim never calls upon his Lord with these words concerning any matter, but his prayer is answered."[281]

Abraham: *"My Lord! Grant me wisdom, and join me with the righteous. Bless me with honorable mention among later generations. Make me one of those awarded the Garden of Bliss. Forgive my father, for he is undoubtedly one of the misguided. And do not disgrace me on the Day all will be resurrected—the Day when neither wealth nor children will be of any benefit."* (Qur'ān 26:83–88)

Moses: *"My Lord! Open up my heart for me, make my task easy, and remove the impediment from my tongue so people may understand my speech."* (Quran 20:25–28). The Prophet Moses made this supplication when God ordered him to go to the tyrant Pharaoh.

---

281. Tirmīdhī, Ḥadīth #3505.

Joseph: *"My Lord, You have given me power and taught me the interpretation of dreams. O Creator of the heavens and the earth, You are my Guardian in this world and the Hereafter! Make me die in submission to You and admit me among the righteous."* (Qur'ān 12:101)

Jesus: *"[O Allāh] If You punish them, they are Your slaves after all. But if You forgive them, You are surely the Almighty, All-Wise."* (Qur'ān 5:118)

Muhammad ﷺ: "O Allāh, I seek refuge in Your pleasure from Your anger and in Your forgiveness from Your punishment, and I seek refuge in You from You. I cannot fully praise You, for You are as You have praised Yourself." (Muslim, Ḥadīth #486).

Chapter 12

WHOM GOD LOVES

"I said to the Lord, 'You promised me that if I followed You, You would walk with me always. But I have noticed that there has only been one set of footprints in the sand during the most trying periods of my life. Why, when I needed you most, have you not been there for me?' The Lord replied, 'During your times of trials and suffering, when you see only one set of footprints, my child, is when I carried you.'" – (Mary Stevenson)[282]

Indeed, long before Mary Stevenson wrote the above lines, God figuratively "carried" us through thick and thin, as He always does. None of us would have survived had it not been for His infinite love.

A heart that God loves is a special heart. He fills such a heart with light, faith, knowledge, and wisdom. He tells angels

---

282. The quote, attributed to Mary Stevenson, has been modified and abridged. For the original version see https://www.footprints-inthe-sand.com/index.php?page=Bio.php.

to love the possessor of such a heart, elevates its ranks, and endears it to posterity. The world remembers people of such hearts with honor and respect and draws inspiration from their noble lives.

Our merciful God loves us all, but some He loves more—those with the purest hearts. Such hearts contain excellence of faith, trust, and patience. They remember God and humble themselves before Him.

The Prophet ﷺ said, "Verily, God does not look at your appearance or wealth, but rather He looks at your hearts and actions."[283] If humanity were to follow God's criterion for love, our world would be a better place, and racism, arrogance, and claims of superiority would seem abhorrent. Then we would measure people's worth in their heart's purity and the excellence of deeds.

The Prophet Muhammad ﷺ once saw a lady prisoner who had lost her infant child in the fog of war. When reunited with her baby, she immediately began to suckle the infant. The Prophet ﷺ turned to his Companions and asked, "Do you think this lady would throw her child in the fire?" When they answered "no," the Prophet ﷺ said, "Allāh is more merciful to his servants than a mother is to her child."[284] One meaning of this ḥadīth is that God does not want to throw anyone into Hell. On the contrary, he looks for every excuse to save them and punishes only those who persist in sins and remain unrepentant to the end.

---

283. Muslim, Ḥadīth #2564.

284. Bukhārī, Ḥadīth #5653, Muslim, Ḥadīth #2754.

God rewards more and punishes less than people deserve as a sign of His mercy. Justice requires that rewards and punishments be proportionate to the actions, but we would be in trouble if God were to apply justice. So instead, God uses His unrivaled generosity in rewarding and uses mercy in punishing. The Qur'ān says, *"Whoever brings a good deed, he should have ten like it, and whoever brings an evil deed, shall be recompensed only with the like of it, and they shall not be dealt with unjustly."* [285]

Ten rewards for one good deed and only one sin for a bad deed show Allāh has set us up for success. Only an enormous amount of sins can cause someone to lose his 10:1 advantage.

The Prophet ﷺ expanded on this verse further, saying, "Whoever intended to perform a good deed but did not do it, Allāh writes it as a good deed. And if he did it, Allāh writes it as from ten good deeds up to seven hundred and multiplied many times. And if he intended to perform an evil deed but did not do it, Allāh writes it as one good deed. And if he did it, then Allāh writes it as one evil deed."[286] This ḥadīth tells us that not acting on an evil thought counts as a good deed with Allāh.

God's love and mercy manifest in two ways, one general and the other special. He is *Ar-Raḥmān* to all his creations but *Ar-Raḥīm* only to believers: *"And your God is one God. There is no deity except Him, the universally merciful [Ar-Raḥmān], the especially merciful [Ar-Raḥīm]."*[287]

---

285. Qur'ān 6:160.

286. Imam an-Nawawi's 40 Ḥadīth, Ḥadīth #37. The Ḥadīth was abridged.

287. Qur'ān 2:163.

To remind believers (and nonbelievers) of this cardinal principle, every chapter of the Qur'ān, except Chapter 9, begins with the phrase, *"In the name of Allāh, the universally merciful, the especially merciful."*

As *Ar-Raḥmān,* He created humans, taught them knowledge, gifted them with lifesaving oxygen, housed them on a hospitable planet, kept that planet at a perfect distance from the sun, and enveloped that planet in the ozone layer to protect them from the sun's ultraviolet rays. Imagine if Earth was a few thousand miles closer or farther from the sun! In the first case, the sun would scorch the planet, and in the second case, it would freeze all life to extinction.

As Ar-Raḥmān, He is merciful not just to humans but to all His creations. Even the birds depend on His benevolence to soar in the sky: *"Do they not see the birds above them outspreading and folding their wings? None holds them aloft except Ar-Raḥmān."* [288]

As *Ar-Raḥīm*, God has an immense affinity with the believers. Many verses in the Qur'ān indicate God's particular regard for them. For example, Chapter 33 says, "*He is especially merciful to the believers.*"[289] Time and time again, the Qur'ān uses the term *Ar-Raḥīm* in the context of believers who rely on Allāh and turn to Him in repentance. Another term that often accompanies *Ar-Raḥīm* is *al-Ghafūr* (the Ever-Forgiving) to assure believers that God will forgive them if they make amends.

---

288. Qur'ān 67:19.

289. Qur'ān 33:43.

God has reserved a special love for:

- the doers of good (2:195);
- the penitent and pure (2:222);
- the pious (3:76);
- the patient (3:146);
- those who rely on God (3:159); and
- the just (49:9).

To this list, we may add the thankful, the truthful, the oath keepers, the trustworthy, the kindhearted, the merciful, and the loving.

Most of these human virtues are a reflection of God's qualities, as evidenced by a ḥadīth that says, "Verily, Allāh created Ādam in His image."[290] According to one opinion, "image" here means Allāh's attributes because the Qur'ān tells us "there is nothing unto like Him" (*laysa kamīth'līhī shay'ūn*).[291]

Therefore, whatever we exemplify of Allāh's attributes is a minuscule fraction of His infinite grace. While Allāh's attributes are eternal and absolute, ours are temporary and relative. Allāh exists of His own power, whereas everything in the universe needs Him to exist. That's why He is *As-Samad*, (Self-Sufficient, Besought), and we are *faqīr* (in need).

290. Muslim, Ḥadīth #2612.

291. Qur'ān 42:11.

The Qur'ān describes this relationship aptly: *"O people, it is you who need Allāh, but Allāh is the Self-Sufficient, worthy of all Praise."*[292]

Although Allāh is our Creator's proper name in Arabic, He has 99 other names called *al-Asmā al-Ḥusna* (The Best Names). These names, in reality, are Allāh's primary attributes but not His only ones. The Qur'ān says, *"And to Allāh belong the best names, so invoke Him by them."*[293] The Prophet ﷺ encouraged Muslims to study and memorize these names because it would help them enter Paradise.[294] Discussing Allāh's 99 attributes is beyond this chapter's scope, but it suffices to say that studying them helps us understand His power and nature and strengthens our hearts. It is a type of *dhikr* which makes our hearts tranquil. Therefore, we should invoke some of these majestic names before asking Allāh for a favor. Wouldn't those seeking favor praise the king before asking? Indeed, Allāh is the Supreme King, and we need to exhibit the best etiquette before Him.

Two Different Loves

There is a fundamental difference between our love for Allāh and His love for us. Many of us love Allāh because we need Him, but Allāh loves us because His love is eternal and the essence of His being. As A. Helwa points out, "love is not something Allāh *does*, love is something Allāh *is*."[295] In *Secrets*

---

292. Qur'ān 35.15.

293. Qur'ān 7:180.

294. Bukhārī, Ḥadīth #6597, Muslim, Ḥadīth #2677.

295. A. Helwa, *Secrets of Divine Love: A Spiritual Journey into the Heart of Islam.* (Nanuet, NY: Naulit Publishing, 2020), 12.

of Divine Love, the author argues that if we are kind, God is kindness; if we are merciful, He is mercy; and peaceful, He is peace (*salām*).

Those who love God know that the sweetness of God's love far surpasses any love. Winning God's love is easy, for it only requires sincere intentions and good works with persistence. The Qur'ān offers a deep insight into qualities that earn someone God's love. Chapter 25, *Al-Furqān* (the Criterion), lays down some traits.

Those God loves walk humbly on earth and respond to rudeness with peace. They spend a good portion of the night prostrating and standing before their Lord, seeking His refuge from Hell. They are neither miserly nor spendthrifts. They do not worship anyone besides the One True God, kill unjustly, or fornicate. If they fall into error but follow up with sincere repentance, the merciful God will overlook their sins and exchange them for good deeds. God's righteous servants do not give false testimony, and when they come across something immoral or evil, they pass it by with dignity. When reminded of God's commands, they do not turn a blind eye or a deaf ear to them. These people ask God to bless them with pious spouses and offspring who will bring joy to their hearts. They also ask God to make them positive role models for the righteous.[296]

God responds to their pure hearts' noble deeds with a promise that He will reward them with lofty mansions in Paradise, where they will abide forever in splendor. They will not have any anxiety, sickness, or even death because they

296. See Qur'ān, Chapter 25, Verses 62–77.

passed the test and earned God's grace. They will receive these bounties because they patiently persevered in worshiping Allāh and doing righteous deeds. We all know how difficult it is to find devotion and solemnity in acts of worship every day amid the chaos of daily life. It burns us out, but worshipers do it with renewed devotion every time.

While God remembers all of us all the time, only the pure-hearted among us remember Him in all circumstances. Such people have *ghīrah*, protective jealousy for their faith, and guard it staunchly. They let faith guide their public and private lives, buying and selling, and worship and recreation. They consider the present life and its challenges as preparation for the Hereafter's blissful life. That's why their first words upon entering Paradise will be, *"Praise to God Who has taken away all anxieties from us, for indeed our Lord is forgiving and ever-appreciative."*[297] How logical their reaction would be, for indeed, this life is full of anxieties from the cradle to the grave, and no one is exempt from them.

None of us can claim Paradise based on virtuous actions alone because our actions are imperfect and too little to earn that eternal and perfect prize. Our good deeds do not equal the favors that Allāh has already granted us in this life. Therefore, the conferment of Paradise is the result of God's mercy and grace. The Prophet ﷺ said to his Companions, "Verily, none of you will enter Paradise by his deeds alone." They said, "Not even you, O Messenger of Allāh?" The Prophet ﷺ said, "Not even I unless Allāh grants me His mercy."[298]

---

297. Qur'ān 35.34.

298. Muslim, Ḥadīth #2818.

An old story illustrates this point well. Among the believing community of a previous nation lived a pious man who devotedly worshiped God for hundreds of years. On Judgment Day, God told him to enter Paradise "through My mercy." The man refused, insisting that he should enter Paradise because of his numerous good deeds. God stopped the man and ordered the angels to put all his virtuous deeds on one scale and his eyesight on another. When the eyesight tipped the balance, the man quickly realized his mistake and begged for entry into Paradise through God's mercy. Indeed the man's heart, mind, and intellect, all gifts from God, would also have outweighed his righteous actions.

Several verses in the Qur'ān appear to say that a person will enter Paradise because of good deeds, like this one: *"Enter Paradise on account of that which you used to do"* (16:32). But this is a misunderstanding. This verse means that righteous actions are a means of getting into Paradise but not enough in themselves. How can finite, imperfect actions ever equal the blessings of an eternal and perfect life where one will never age, be sick or sad, or die? However, out of God's love and generosity, He rewards our good works with something immensely better, which we neither deserved nor earned based on our actions alone.

Why Do We Worship?

People worship God for different reasons. Some worship Him because of their fear of Hell, others to get into Paradise, yet others out of sheer love for God. All three are valid reasons for worshiping our Creator, although opinions vary as to which is more admirable.

Fear

The Arabic word *taqwā* appears nearly 119 times in the Qur'ān. Some translate it as fear or consciousness of Allāh. In this section, I shall discuss *taqwā* in the context of fear. Many verses in the Qur'ān tell us to fear Allāh and the Day of Judgment, addressing both believers and the rest of humanity. For example:

"Fear the Day when you shall all be returned to God; then every soul shall be paid in full what it has earned, and they shall not be wronged" (2:281).

According to the majority opinion, this is the last revealed verse of the Qur'ān. Given that there will never be a direct revelation from God after this verse, the command to fear Allāh takes on a special significance in the same way as the parting advice we give to our family is most memorable.

Then there are verses that raise the specter of fear from other angles, such as *"And guard yourselves against the Fire prepared for the unbelievers"* (3:131) and *"Fear God! God is severe in punishment"* (5:2). Finally, the Qur'ān issues a general warning: *"O humanity, fear your Lord. The catastrophe of the Last Hour shall be dreadful indeed"* (22:1).

In the Prophet Zechariah's story in Chapter 21, Allāh describes him and his wife as those who used to "call upon Us with hope and fear, and they were humble" (21:90). Hope and fear are running themes in the Qur'ān. While in Arabic, hope translates as *rajā* and fear *khashī'ah*, respectively, in the Qur'ānic terminology, they are called *targhīb* and *tarhīb*. Through *targhīb*, Allāh encourages people to believe in Him and do righteous deeds to earn Paradise. Through *tarhīb*, He threatens them with Hell when they reject Him.

Fearing Allāh, as the Prophet Zechariah did, was normative for all of God's prophets, including the Prophet Muhammad, ﷺ who told his Companions that he was the most God-fearing among them. He considered consciousness or fear of God so critical that he began his speeches with three verses that urged people to be conscious of their Lord whenever he addressed them. These verses form part of what is known as *khutbah al-haājah* (the sermon of necessity).

1) *"O you who have faith, fear Allāh as it is His right to be feared and do not die unless you are Muslims."* (3:102)

2) *"Fear Allāh, in Whose name you ask each other, and honor your family ties, for Allāh is ever watchful over you."* (4:1)

3) *"Fear Allāh and say what is right. He will set right your deeds for you and forgive your sins. Whoever obeys Allāh and His Messenger has achieved a great triumph."* (33:70–71)

The Prophet ﷺ said, "Nobility is in fear of Allāh."[299] One of his famous Companions, ʿAbdullāh ibn Masʿūd, equated knowledge with the fear of Allāh, saying, "Knowledge is not knowing many narrations. Verily, knowledge is the fear of Allāh."[300] Hasan al-Basri, the prodigious Successor, considered fear of Allāh as the gateway to good conduct. A believer, he

299. Tirmidhī, Ḥadīth #3271.

300. Rawḍat al-ʿUqalā, #9.

said, "does not increase in piety and righteousness unless he increases in fear."[301]

Some of God's noble worshipers are the scholars who fear their Lord and draw closer to Him through knowledge and righteous deeds. Allāh confirms that this group fears the Divine: *"Only those of His servants, who possess the knowledge, truly fear God."*[302]

Paradise

The Qur'ān encourages us to seek Paradise, whose grandeur and splendor are unparalleled and which, the Prophet ﷺ said, no eye has ever seen, ear has ever heard, and no heart has ever imagined.[303] Then he recited a verse from the Qur'ān: *"No soul can imagine what delights are kept in store for them as a reward for what they used to do."*[304]

We all love to have a good life, and nothing magnifies it as well as Paradise. Worshiping God to earn Paradise does not trivialize our good deeds. Quite the contrary, God encourages us to seek Paradise, using three verses of the Qur'ān to emphasize its urgency.

The first one says, "*And compete (sābiqū) with one another for forgiveness from your Lord and a Paradise as vast as the heavens and the earth, prepared for those who believe in Allāh and His messengers. This is the favor of Allāh, which He grants to whomever He wills. And Allāh is*

301. Siyar A'lām al-Nubalā,' #4/586.

302. Qur'ān 35:28.

303. Muslim, Ḥadīth #6781.

304. Qur'ān 32:17.

the Lord of infinite bounty."[305] This verse incentivizes worship and clarifies that God grants Paradise from His grace. Our good deeds alone do not entitle us to it.

The second verse says, "*And hasten (sāriʿū) to forgiveness from your Lord and a garden as wide as the heavens and earth, prepared for the righteous.*"[306]

And the third verse uses *sāriʿū*, a term that means hastening to the point of running. Another verse makes it even more urgent: "*And so run to Allāh! Indeed I am a plain warner to you from Him.*"[307] It means to run away from Satan and sins to the ever-present refuge of Allāh. It is an amazing concept that God is our final refuge, even when we anger Him, because no one can shelter us against His wrath except He. The Qur'ān aptly describes this ultimate amnesty in the verse that says, "*There is no refuge from Allāh except in Him.*"[308]

Another verse mentions something more supreme than the delights of Paradise: Allāh's pleasure. "Allāh has promised the believing men and women Gardens under which rivers flow, to stay there forever, and magnificent homes in the Gardens of Eternity, and—above all—the pleasure of Allāh. That is truly the ultimate triumph" (9:72). So, the "ultimate triumph" (*fawzun ʿadhīm*) is not Paradise; it is Allāh's happiness with the inhabitants of Paradise, whose ultimate manifestation is seeing Allāh.

---

305. Qur'ān 57:21.

306. Qur'ān 3:133.

307. Qur'ān 51:50.

308. Qur'ān 9:118.

A ḥadīth says that every reward in Paradise will pale compared to seeing God. "When the people of Paradise enter it, Allāh Almighty will say: 'Would you like anything more?' They will say: 'Have you not brightened our faces? Have you not admitted us into Paradise and saved us from Hellfire?' Then, Allāh will lift the veil, and nothing they received will be more beloved to them than looking at their Lord Almighty."[309] The Prophet ﷺ then recited a verse that translates as *"Those who do good will have the finest reward and even more."* [310]

The Prophet ﷺ himself asked for Paradise: "O Allāh, I ask of You for Paradise."[311] He told Muʿādh Ibn Jabal, "Paradise has one hundred levels, and between every two levels is like the distance between the heavens and earth. *Al-Firdaws* is its highest level, from which four rivers of Paradise flow, and above which is the Throne [of Allāh]. When you ask Allāh, ask for *Al-Firdaws*."[312]

Worshiping Allāh to attain Paradise, therefore, does not belittle our worship. Indeed, He orders us to seek Paradise through worship, even if worship alone is insufficient to enter the heavenly abode.

309. Muslim, Ḥadīth #181.

310. Qur'ān 10:26.

311. Ibn Mājah, Vol 2. Ḥadīth #327.

312. Mūsnad Aḥmad, Ḥadīth #22232.

Love

Loving someone who loves you more, like your mother, seems logical. So, what about Allāh's unfathomable love and kindness for us? It makes far more sense to worship Allāh out of love, for He is infinitely loving.

Muslim scholars believe that loving Allāh is incumbent upon believers. The following verse supports that premise: *"Say, O Prophet, "If your parents, children, siblings, spouses, extended family, the wealth you have acquired and the trade whose decline you fear, and the homes you cherish—if these are more beloved to you than Allāh and His Messenger, and struggling in His Way, then wait until Allāh brings His Judgment. Allāh does not guide the rebellious people."*"[313]

One of Allāh's names is *al-Wadūd*, the One who is full of pure love, but Allāh is more than just the One Who loves His creation. He is the source of love. The word *al-Wadūd* appears twice in the Qur'ān, both times combined with mercy and forgiveness: "*Indeed My Lord is especially merciful and most loving*" (11:90) and "*And He is most forgiving and most loving*" (85:14). According to one opinion, this combination indicates that Allāh forgives due to His mercy and accepts His servants' obedience due to love.[314]

The Prophet ﷺ said, "Allāh has divided mercy into one hundred parts; He retained with Him ninety-nine parts and sent down to earth one part. Through this one part, creatures

313. Qur'ān 9:24.

314. Sharh as-mā al-Husnā (Explanation of Allah's Beautiful Names), vol. 2. (Karachi: Pakistan, House of Knowledge Trust, 2009), 24.

deal with one another with compassion, so much so that an animal lifts its hoof over its young lest it should hurt it."[315]

A ḥadīth also says that "When Allāh completed the creation, He wrote in His Book which is with Him on His throne, 'My mercy overcomes My anger.'"[316]

The following verse is further proof that worshiping Allāh out of love is required from us: *"O believers, Whoever among you abandons their faith, Allāh will replace them with others who love Him and Whom He loves."* [317]

Worship, as a rule, should be a labor of love. But some argue that sheer love should be the highest–nay the *only*–motivation for worshiping Allāh, for that is, in their estimation, the highest form of reverence. Being saved from Hell and admitted into Paradise is a byproduct of loving Allāh.

Rābiʿa al-ʿAdawiyya, the famous mystic from Basra, said: "O Allāh, if I worship You for fear of Hell, burn me in Hell, and if I worship You in the hope of Paradise, exclude me from Paradise. But if I worship You only for Your Own sake, then do not deny me Your everlasting beauty."[318]

Muhammad Iqbal, the renowned twentieth-century philosopher-poet of India, rebuked Muslims for treating God's

---

315. Bukhārī, Ḥadīth #5654, Muslim, Ḥadīth #2752.

316. Bukhārī, Ḥadīth #3194.

317. Qur'ān 5:54.

318. Farid al-Din Attar, Muslim Saints and Mystics: Episodes from the Tadhkirat al-Auliya' (Memorial of the Saints), transl. A.J. Arberry (Chicago, IL: University of Chicago Press, 1966), 51.

worship like some business deal. In his 1924 poem, Bāng-e-Darā (the Call of the Marching Bell), he said:

It is worship, not trade
O ignorant, wish not for reward

The Prophet Muhammad ﷺ praised a supplication of Prophet David, who used to pray, "O Allāh, I ask You for Your love and the love of those who love You and the deeds that will bring me Your love. O Allāh, make Your love more beloved to me than myself and my family."[319]

While the love of Allāh should be intrinsic to our worship, the Qur'ān repeatedly reminds us that fear of Allāh and yearning for Paradise must also be a part of it. To love Allāh is to obey Him, and He has commanded us to worship Him out of love, fear, and hope. When we love Allāh, He will pull us out of every difficulty in this life, save us from Hell, and grant us His vision in Paradise.

The Prophet ﷺ said that in the Hereafter, "You will be with those you love."[320] The Prophet's ﷺ statement mirrors the verse that says, *"And whoever obeys Allāh and the Messenger will be in the company of those blessed by Allāh: the prophets, the people of truth, the martyrs, and the righteous—what honorable company!"* [321]

319. Tirmīdhī, Ḥadīth #3490.

320. Bukhārī, Hadith #3435, Muslim, Hadith #2639.

321. Qur'ān 4:69.

Chapter 13

HEARTS THAT REMEMBER DEATH

"The death you are running away from will inevitably come to you. Then you will be returned to the Knower of the unseen and the seen, and He will inform you of what you used to do." – (Qur'ān 62:8)

A believer's heart is always conscious of the inevitability of death. Dying is nothing but the fulfillment of God's decree: *"Every soul shall taste death."* [322] There is no place to hide or run away from death, not even in "fortified towers,"[323] as the Qur'ān says. Even the Angel of Death will die one day.

Everyone dislikes death, but Islam teaches us to remember death to prepare for the next life. The Prophet ﷺ said, "Remember often the destroyer of pleasures."[324] He meant this life's pleasures because, for a righteous person, real and

322. Qur'ān 3:185.

323. Qur'ān 4:78.

324. Tirmīdhī, Hadith# 2307.

everlasting pleasure will begin only after death. So, death is a harbinger of good news for the righteous.

Death is a painful reality, but the righteous think of it as a deterrent against heedlessness, like the Islamic punishment of "life for a life" (*qīṣāṣ*) is a deterrent against murder. Allāh called the punishment for murder life-giving: *"In the law of retaliation, there is life for you, o people of understanding so that you may become God-fearing."*[325]

While there will be murder despite capital punishment, some argue that the rate of homicide is generally lower under capital punishment laws. The threat of severe consequences, they contend, would make the would-be murderer think twice and thus spare his life and the life of his victim.

In Islam, not all death is equal. Death for the martyr (*shahīd*) is sweet, something he would wish to return to this world to experience again and again. Also, death is not the end of everything. As Iqbal, the poet, said in a beautiful couplet,

Death is a renewal in the way of living,
Behind the sleep's veil lies awakening

Some deaths have far-reaching consequences. The death of the Prophet Muhammad ﷺ was extremely hard for his Companions. In their sincere love and zeal for him, they did not envision their Prophet ﷺ ever leaving them. That's why when he died, they were devastated, with 'Umar threatening to kill anyone who said the Prophet ﷺ had passed away. It had to

325. Qur'ān 2.179.

be Abu Bakr to calm 'Umar and soothe others. He proclaimed that the Prophet ﷺ had indeed died, but Allāh is ever-living,[326] and then recited: *"Muhammad is but a messenger; other messengers have gone before him. Would you return to disbelief if he were to die or be killed? Those who do so will not harm Allāh whatsoever. And Allāh will reward those who are grateful."* [327] The Qur'ān includes other forewarnings of the Prophet's ﷺ demise, for instance: "*O Prophet, You will die, and they too will die.*"[328]

The Prophet ﷺ himself told his Companions that his death would be the biggest tragedy to befall them.[329] Anas ibn Mālik, his servant, said, "Never did I see a day more beautiful or bright than the day the Messenger ﷺ entered Medina, and I witnessed his death, and I did not see a day darker or more hideous than the day the Messenger ﷺ died."[330] Aside from the Prophet's ﷺ death shattering his family and Companions' hearts, the Muslims of future generations can never recover from his loss. One way to understand this loss is through inter-Muslim groupings and religious sectarianism. Had the Prophet ﷺ been alive today, he would rectify our beliefs and reconcile our differences. Moreover, the believers would not be divided and fight each other.

The righteous do not despise death. They know that death announces the coming of a suffering-free life of eternity. The Prophet ﷺ captured this reality when he said, "The world is

---

326. Bukhārī, Ḥadīth #3667, 3668.

327. Qur'ān 3:144.

328. Qur'ān 39:30.

329. Ibn Mājah, Ḥadīth #1300.

330. Mūsnad Ahmad, Ḥadīth #3:122.

a prison for the believer and Paradise for the disbeliever."[331] A believer shuns the unlawful pleasures of this life in return for unlimited superior rewards in the Hereafter. God tests our obedience in this life by imposing restrictions on the faithful. A believer observes God's limits (ḥudūd) and begs forgiveness when they make a mistake. The Prophet ﷺ taught the Companions a powerful prayer and called it Master Supplication (*Sayyid al-Istīghfār*): "O Allāh! You are my Lord! None has the right to be worshipped but You. You created me, and I am Your slave, and I am faithful to my covenant and promise as much as I can. I seek refuge with You from all the evil I have done. I acknowledge before You all the blessings You have bestowed upon me, and I confess to You all my sins. So I implore You to forgive my sins, for nobody can forgive sins except You."[332]

A believer fasts during Ramadan while others around him enjoy food and drink. They leave their warm beds at dawn to pray while others sleep, and they forsake unlawful pleasures while others indulge. A disbeliever, on the other hand, does not refrain from anything. They think there is only one life to live and, therefore, they must enjoy it to the fullest. They obey man's laws for fear of imprisonment but ignore the laws of God because they do not believe in Him and do not fear any reckoning.

It makes sense that when God sets up the court on Judgment Day, He will reward the believers with something better than

---

331. Muslim, Ḥadīth #2956.

332. Bukhārī, Hadith #318, Tīrmīdhī, Hadith #3393, Nasā'ī, Hadith #5522, Ahmad, Hadith #16662.

what they shunned in this life for His sake while punishing the disbelievers for their defiance.

The Prophet ﷺ showed the right priorities for this life and the next. Just days before he died, in the middle of the night, the Prophet ﷺ called for Abu Muwayhibah, his freedman, to take him to the cemetery to pray for the martyrs. After supplication, the Prophet ﷺ turned to Abu Muwayhibah and said, "I have been given the choice between the keys of the treasures of this world and long life here followed by Paradise, and meeting my Lord and Paradise (right away)."[333] Abu Muwayhibah quickly advised the Prophet ﷺ to choose the former, but the Prophet ﷺ replied he had already chosen the latter, meaning to depart now.

The Prophet ﷺ led the dawn prayer the next day. After he had finished, he mounted the pulpit and invoked Allāh's blessings on the martyrs of Uhud for a long time, as if this were his last opportunity to do so. Then he broke the previous night's news to the congregation: "Allāh has given one of His servants a choice between this world and that which is with Allāh, and he has chosen the latter."[334]

On the day the Prophet ﷺ died, the last words he said were, "With those on whom You have bestowed Your Grace, with the prophets and the truthful, the martyrs and the good-doers. O Allāh, forgive me, have mercy upon me, and join me with the Companionship on high."[335] It was similar to a revelation Allāh sent to him: *"And whoever obeys Allāh and the Messenger, then*

---

333. Ibn Ishāq, Sirāt Rasul Allāh.

334. Ibid.

335. Ibid.

they will be in the company of those on whom Allāh has bestowed His grace, of the prophets, the truthful, the martyrs, and the righteous. And how excellent are these Companions!" [336]

One should take heart that Allāh promises to unite all righteous people in Paradise: *"And those who believed and whose descendants followed them in faith, We will join with them their descendants, and We will not deprive them of anything of their deeds."*[337]

While death is an indisputable truth, the hearts of the righteous see it as a gateway to meeting their Lord, as the Prophet's ﷺ heart did. He shunned the riches of this world and preferred to unite with the *source* of all riches. He told us, "Whoever loves to meet Allāh, Allāh loves to meet him."[338]

According to an ancient story, when the Angel of Death came to the Prophet Abraham, he said, "Allāh has commanded me to take your soul!" The latter responded, "What kind of friend takes his friend's soul?" At that moment, Allāh revealed to the Prophet Abraham, "And what kind of friend does not want to meet his friend?"[339] In Islamic tradition, Allāh took two close friends (*khalīl*) from this world—the prophets Abraham and Muhammad ﷺ.

Because death is inevitable doesn't mean we sit around and wait to die. That would make life agonizing because we would withdraw from life and only think of death. How great that God does not tell us the time of our death!

---

336. Nisaa 4:69.

337. Qur'ān 52.21

338. Muslim, Ḥadīth #157.

339. Related by Imām al-Qurtubī in al-Tadkhīra, according to American scholar Suhaib Webb.

Other hearts want to enjoy this life to the fullest and forget death exists. The pagans of Mecca used to tell the Prophet ﷺ, *"There is nothing beyond the life of this world. We die; others are born. And nothing destroys us but time."*[340] Because they did not believe in the resurrection and accountability, and to them, life meant pursuing their whims and desires. For them, death was a dead end. Nihilists, who reject all religious and moral principles, often face depression because, in their view, there is nothing to aspire to in a universe and life that have no purpose.

So the believers' hearts long for a delightful experience when they awake in the next realm. A ḥadīth offers an exhilarating glimpse of what awaits. The Prophet ﷺ said,

> Verily, when the believing servant is leaving this life and journeying to the Hereafter, angels will descend upon him; their faces will be radiant as if they were suns, and they will have a shroud and an embalmment with them from Paradise. Then, they will sit within eyeshot of him. Then the angel of death will come and sit at his head and say, "O you righteous soul; come out to forgiveness and pleasure from your Lord." So it will come out like a drop of water comes out of the mouth of a jug, then he will take it, not leaving it in his hand for longer than the blink of an eye until they (he and the other angels) have placed it in that shroud and that embalmment. A fragrant smell will emanate from it like that of the most sweet-smelling musk on the face of the earth. Then they shall ascend with it and not pass by any group of angels, but they will ask: "Who is this good and sweet-smelling soul?" Then they shall say to them (he is) the son of so and so,

340. Qur'ān 45:24.

recalling the best names he used to be called in this life. When they reach the lowest heaven and ask permission to enter, entry is granted up to the seventh heaven. Then Allāh, the exalted and high, shall say: "Write the deeds of my servant in'Illīyīn.[341] It shall be said, "Return him to the earth, for I have created them from it, return them to it, and resurrect them from it." So his soul is returned to his body, and he will hear the footsteps of his friends who buried him when they leave him.

Then two severe angels shall come and sit him up next to them and ask him: "Who is your Lord?" He shall reply, "My Lord is Allāh." Then they shall ask him: "What is your religion?" He shall answer: "My religion is Islam." Then they shall ask him, "Who is your prophet?" He shall answer: "He is Muhammad ﷺ, the Messenger of Allāh." Then a caller will call from the heaven: "My slave has spoken the truth, so spread out for him furnishings from the heaven, and clothe him from the heaven, and open a door for him (within his grave) from the heaven." So its goodness and smell will reach him, and his grave will be expanded for him as far as he can see.

Then a person with a handsome face, fine clothes, and a sweet smell will come to him and say: "I bring you glad tidings of that which will make you happy." The man will say, "Who are you? for your face is that of someone who brings good news." He shall reply: "I am your good deeds." Then the man will say, "My Lord let the Last Hour come so I may go to my family and my wealth."[342]

---

341. 'Illīyīn is a register of good people. (Qur'ān 83:18)

342. Bukhārī, Part 2, p. 478, Ahkām al-Janā'iz. This Ḥadīth has more than one narrator with slightly different wordings.

The ḥadīth continues and describes the dreadful things that will happen to those who consciously and persistently reject God's message.

In more than one place, the Qur'ān informs us that God and His angels will help the goodhearted soul at the time of death: *"Surely those who say, 'Our Lord is Allāh,' and then remain steadfast, the angels descend upon them at the time of death, saying, 'Do not fear, nor grieve. Instead, rejoice in the good news of Paradise promised to you. We were your supporters in this worldly life and will be in the Hereafter. There you will have whatever your souls desire, and you ask for: a rich provision from the All-Forgiving, Especially Merciful Lord"* (41:30–32).

One of the terrifying experiences in the grave will be the three questions mentioned in the above ḥadīth. Although the Prophet ﷺ told us the answers, they cannot be memorized and repeated just like that. However, the believers should rejoice that God will help them at that moment. The Qur'ān says: "*God will strengthen the believers with a steadfast word, in the present life and the Hereafter*" (14:27). Muslim commentators of the Qur'ān explain that steadfastness in this world and the Hereafter means that God will help us stay on a righteous course in the earthly life and pass the grave's test, which is a stepping stone into the Hereafter.

An interesting point here is that the death we think of is the second death. None of us remembers the first death because we do not know about it except subconsciously. We may call the first death pre-creation or primordial existence. We find a reference to this death in the Qur'ān where the sinners will plead with God on Judgment Day, saying, *"Our Lord, twice You caused us to die, and twice You gave us life. We now admit our sins. Is there a way out [of the punishment]?"* (40:11). Scholars say that the first death is the soul without a body, and the first life is when God's angel breathes the soul into the fetus. The second death is when the soul leaves the earthly body, and the second life is the resurrection. In a fascinating story from the Qur'ān, God asked every soul before He joined it with the earthly body, *"Am I not your Lord?"*[343] Without fail, every soul had affirmed Allāh's lordship.

The righteous and wise people remain mindful of death because death will prevent them from earning any more good deeds, except a continuous charity they may leave behind, like beneficial knowledge, works of a public good, and pious children who would pray for them. Death also, without exception, will terminate a chance for repentance.

On Judgment Day, the righteous will be in for a pleasant surprise to find large amounts of good deeds they did not recall doing, only to discover they are the reward of the continuous charity they left behind. On the other hand, the tyrants will find themselves in a deeper abyss because of the legacy of their sins and oppression. They will sorely regret their sins and beg to come back to Earth to make amends but will find it impossible to return to their previous lives.

In the ancient story of Pharaoh, just before he drowned, he attempted to submit to One True God.[344] And the Divine's answer came. *"Now?! But you always disobeyed and were one of the*

---

343. Qur'ān 7:172.

344. Qur'ān 10:90.

corruptors."[345] Pharaoh's story is a potent reminder that when the stupor of death seizes a person, the door of repentance shuts for him. Pharaoh will lead his disbelieving people into the Fire in the Hereafter.

Hearts that remember death keep things in perspective. Muslims involved in *da'wah* (calling others to Islam) often tell their young trainees that they are like passengers in a train station's waiting room. It won't be long before their train pulls into the platform, and they leave. It would make no sense for the passengers to get too absorbed in the waiting room's decor. So, life is like a journey, and we are the passengers. We spend only a short time at the station and leave when the train arrives. The train of life is death.

The Prophet ﷺ once took hold of the shoulders of a young Companion, Abdullah ibn 'Umar, and said, "Be in this world as if you were a stranger or a traveler along a path."[346] It is profound advice, which he applied to himself, saying, "Verily, the example of this world and myself is that of a rider who seeks shade under a tree, then he moves on and leaves it [behind]."[347] The Prophet's ﷺ gesture to Ibn 'Umar made the advice highly personal and underscored its importance.

A traveler only needs what is essential. Too much baggage will slow him down, and only righteousness is the best provision for the one whose destination is the Hereafter. There is no need to take things that won't help on the journey. The Qur'ān tells pilgrims to God's house in Mecca: *"Take necessary provisions for*

---

345. Qur'ān 10:91.

346. Bukhārī, Ḥadīth #6053.

347. Musnad Ahmad, Ḥadīth #3701

the journey—indeed, the best provision is righteousness." [348] When the verse came down, pilgrimage (*Ḥajj*) from Medina took weeks. People bade farewell to their families as if they were going on a trip of no return. Indeed, some died during the pilgrimage.

Before the Battle of the Confederates, the Prophet ﷺ joined his Companions in digging a trench to protect their city from a large invading force. Here he was, a prophet of God, covered in dust without any pretense of greatness, working like any other person. So moved, the Companions chanted words of praise and support for their prophet, to which he reciprocated: "O Allāh, there is no true life except the life of the Hereafter. Forgive the Anṣār and the Muhājirūn."[349] The Prophet's ﷺ prayer greatly soothed the Companions' hearts and reminded them about the right priorities.

The Companions remembered death to keep their pursuit of this world in check. They thoroughly understood the Qur'ān's clear warning for those who run after this fleeting earthly life and forget death: *"Competition for more and more distracted you [from God's remembrance] till you reached the grave."*[350]

God, Who created life and death, has appointed an angel to take the soul of every person. These angels will keep coming back until the last of us remains, and that is a reality no heart can deny, not even the one that does not believe in life after death. Therefore, the righteous remember death with fear and hope. It is the perfect combination because we all sin and hope that the Most Merciful will forgive us.

---

348. Qur'ān 2:197.

349. Bukhārī, Ḥadīth #2679, Muslim, Ḥadīth #1805.

350. Qur'ān 102:1–2.

What buoys the righteous hearts is Allāh's promise of a graceful end to this life. The angel of death will appear to them in a pleasant form, offering comfort during distress. And Allāh will say to them, *"O tranquil soul! Return to your Lord, well pleased with Him and well-pleasing to Him. So join My servants, and enter My Paradise."* It would be a far cry from the unrighteous's end, whose souls the angel of death will extract with great violence: *"If you could only see the wrongdoers in the throes of death while the angels are stretching out their hands, saying, "Give up your souls! Today you will be rewarded with the torment of disgrace for telling lies about Allāh and for being arrogant toward His revelations!"*[351]

For the hearts that remember death, hope to meet Allāh, and are in awe of His Majesty, Allāh promises them a double reward: *"And whoever feared standing before their Lord will have two Gardens."*[352]

The righteous hearts look at this world's transient life as a test and a passthrough for the life of eternal salvation and happiness. God has already cut a deal with them. The Qur'ān says, *"Allāh has indeed purchased their lives and wealth from the believers in exchange for Paradise."*[353]

Hasan al-Basri's advice evoked the above verse when he said, "Sell this life for the next, and you win both. Sell the next life for this, and you lose both."

351. Qur'ān 6:93.

352. Qur'ān 55:46.

353. Qur'ān 9:111.

Chapter 14

REVIVING THE HEART

"He is the One Who sent down serenity upon the hearts of the believers so that they may increase even more in their faith." – (Qur'ān 48:4)

Our hearts constantly require care and spiritual revival. The physical heart, when neglected or abused, dies of cardiac diseases. Heart ailments are the leading cause of death in the United States, where one person dies every thirty-six seconds due to cardiovascular disease.[354] As a spiritual entity, the heart constantly struggles to push away Satanic whispers and evil inclinations of the soul that make it sick or, in worst cases, cause its demise.

The physical heart works tirelessly from the moment it springs to life within six weeks of pregnancy until the soul leaves the body. It beats about 100,000 times a day, 2.5 billion times in an average lifespan. As a result, it pumps approximately 1 million barrels of blood during our lifetime. That's enough to

---

354. 1. "Underlying Causes of Death, 1999–2019," Centers for Disease Control and Prevention, last accessed March 23, 2021, https://wonder.cdc.gov/ucd-icd10.html.

fill more than three supertankers.[355] The vascular system that sends this life-giving blood is over 60,000 miles long, more than two times Earth's circumference. Interestingly, the heart starts beating before the brain's formation without any central nervous system.

Alas, the spiritual heart, the overlooked essence deep inside that "lump of flesh," determines our salvation or damnation. Unlike God, Who perceives all, we cannot *see* the spiritual heart, but we may undoubtedly experience it. "God's Hand" is visible everywhere and in everything to the discerning eyes. So too, are the inner workings of the spiritual heart. Like all created living things, the spiritual heart requires nourishment to stay healthy and treatment when it becomes sick.

Reviving the spiritual heart is crucial for two reasons. One, God will take the heart into account on Judgment Day: "*Indeed, the hearing, the sight, and the heart, [God) will question you about them.*"[356]

The reason for this questioning is twofold. Firstly, God has loaned our faculties to us. We are only trustees or caretakers, and the owner has every right to question how we used His entrustments. When we do righteous deeds, thanks and praise are ultimately due to the One who created the faculties we used to perform those deeds, not ourselves. If we misuse those faculties, it is a sign of ungratefulness and a breach of contract. The heart is God's creation, so it is only fitting that the heart should thank its Creator.

---

355. "Amazing Heart Facts," Nova Online, last accessed March 21, 2021, https://www.pbs.org/wgbh/nova/heart/heartfacts.html.

356. Qur'ān 17:36.

Secondly, God said He would admit into Paradise "Those who bring a pure heart"[357] and those who are "righteous" (*al-muttaqūn*).[358] Both the pure-hearted and the righteous-hearted have one thing in common: they guard against corruption and remain mindful of God's presence. It is not that these people never sin because to sin is human. Instead, their hearts blamed them when they erred, prompting them to repent swiftly. Therefore, on Judgment Day, God will honor the people of the "pure heart" (*qalbun salīm*) and the "self-reproaching hearts" (*qalbun munīb*).

"And Paradise will be brought near to the righteous remaining no longer far away [A caller will say] 'This is what you were promised. [A promise] for everyone who returned to God and kept their covenant; Who feared the Merciful God, though He is unseen; And came to Him with a penitent heart.'" [359]

Sickness and Cure

Our hearts can and do become spiritually sick, and there are ways to recognize when they are sick. The most significant sign that a heart is sick is when it does not know its Creator and cannot tell right from wrong. In a fascinating story from the Qur'ān, God asks every soul before He joins it with the earthly body, "Am I not your Lord?"[360] Without fail, every single soul affirms Allāh's Lordship. The rationale behind the oath was to implant awareness of a Creator in the subconsciousness of the creation. Therefore, God-consciousness is in our innate nature

---

357. Qur'ān 26:89–90.

358. Qur'ān 15:45.

359. Qur'ān 26:30–33.

360. Qur'ān 7:172.

(*fiṭrah*), our DNA, and to reject God is to defy a cardinal truth that our inner self attests. *Fiṭrah,* which God has embedded in us, is different from intellect, which we acquire later in life. A person accepts the existence of God naturally but rejects Him due to flawed intellect.

The Qur'ān also says that Allāh inspired the soul with the ability to distinguish right from wrong.[361] Due to this consciousness, when we want to do something wrong, we find resistance within ourselves. And when we do sin, it bothers us, and we wish our sins to remain hidden from people and not cause us embarrassment. For this reason, the Qur'ān teaches us to ask God to forgive our sins and hide them from others: *"Our Lord, forgive us our sins and cover our evil deeds [from people] and cause us to die with the righteous."*[362]

Our primordial affirmation of a Supreme Creator Who has made *good* distinct from *evil* is part of our Adamic predisposition and consciousness. The spiritual heart recognizes God's right to be worshiped exclusively, but doubts, transgression, and hedonism suppress the heart's native instincts. At this point, the spiritual heart becomes like a person whose mind is impaired from intoxicants or like a GPS that has lost the satellite signal. When we forget God, we lose sight of the purpose of our creation. Just as a drunkard sees reality after regaining his sobriety, a heart sees its wrongs upon regaining God-consciousness.

---

361. Qur'ān 91:8.

362. Qur'ān 3:193.

The Qur'ān says about persistent sinners, *"No! Their deeds have cast a veil over their hearts."*[363] The dark veil of sins prevents the light of faith from entering the heart like thick clouds prevent the sunlight from illuminating the Earth. The sun shines every day without fail, even if we cannot see it due to cloudy weather. Similarly, the heart knows its Creator and wants to obey Him even if the sins temporarily dim that cognition.

Interestingly, one of the meanings of *insān* (human) is forgetful, which comes from its derivative *nasya,* meaning forgot. This is an important point because forgetting is different from denying. A person may forget or ignore the divine purpose behind his creation—such as resurrection, Judgment Day, accountability—but his *fiṭrah* does not deny it.

As mentioned earlier, Ibn Taymiyah calls desires and doubts the mother of all spiritual heart diseases.[364] He deems the cognizance of the "truth" that we exist to worship God a prerequisite for the heart's revival. This opinion springs from the Qur'ānic verse, *"I created the jinn*[365] *and humankind only that they might worship Me."*[366]

His famous student, Ibn al-Qayyim al-Jawziyah, said, "The heart has six places in which it roams . . . . Three of these are lowly and three lofty. The lowly is a world that entices it, an ego that nags at it, and a foe who seductively whispers to it. The

---

363. Qur'ān 83:14.

364. Ahmad Ibn Taymiyyah, *Diseases of the Hearts and Their Cures*, trans. Abu Rumaysah. (Birmingham, UK: Dar-us-Sunnah, 2000), 41.

365. In Islam, jinns are invisible creatures, like angels. While God created angels from light, He created jinns from a smokeless fire. Another quality that separates jinns from angels is that they have free will, like humans.

366. Qur'ān 51:56.

three lofty things are knowledge by which it gains clarity, an intellect that guides it, and a deity [God] to which it is devoted in worship. So these are the places wherein hearts wander."[367]

According to Ibn al-Qayyim, "If the heart is nourished upon God's remembrance (*dhīkr*), quenched with meditation (*tafakkūr*) and cleansed of blemishes (*ʿoyūb*), it will witness great wonders and be infused with deep wisdom."[368]

Al-Ghazālī said that some knowledge of the heart's spiritual diseases is required to rid oneself of them. Like ʿUmar ibn al-Khaṭṭāb's statement that one needs to know the evil to guard against it. Once we know our malaise, we must attempt to treat it. The Qur'ān links success to cleansing the soul: *"Successful indeed are those who purify their souls, and doomed are those that corrupt it."* [369]

The Prophet Muhammad ﷺ said, "There is no disease that Allāh has created, except that He also has created its treatment."[370] The best news for those who suffer from spiritual heart disease is that the door of its revival is wide open until the very end. In His infinite mercy, God does not consign a person to Hell at the commission of the first sin but instead grants him the opportunity to repent until before the pangs of death overtake him.

Among Allāh's names are the Guide *(al-Hādi)* and the Bestower of Faith *(al-Mu'min)*. He continues to guide people

---

367. Al-Jawziyyah, Ibn al-Qayyim, *Zād al-Maʿād fī Hadyi Khayr al-ʿIbād. Eds. Shuʿaib al-Arnaʾūṭ and ʿAbd al-Qādir al-Arnaʾūṭ*. Trans. by Mikail ibn Mahboob Ariff (Beirut: Mu'assasah al-Risālah, 1998), 24–25.

368. Ibid.

369. Qur'ān 91:9–10.

370. Bukhārī, Vol. 7, Book 71, Ḥadīth #582.

into faith and righteousness as long as they repent and beg for His mercy.

The Prophet Muhammad ﷺ taught that a person's last actions determine his status with God. Therefore, like an admissions office that considers the applicant's highest SAT score and ignores the inferior ones, God may choose our best actions and ignore those that fall short.

While to err is human and to forgive divine, God encourages sinners to break free from the prison of sins through the Qur'ān and the Sunnah of His prophet. However, it wouldn't be fair to forgive those who never expressed remorse for sins, never tried to make amends, or sought forgiveness. Ignoring and trivializing sins leads to more sins, ultimately making the heart heedless.

ʿAbdullāh ibn Judʿān was among the noblest in the pre-Islamic Meccan society, and his generosity, sense of justice, and kindness were legendary. He was a distant great-uncle of ʿĀyeshah, the Prophet's ﷺ wife.

ʿĀyeshah once asked, "O Messenger of Allāh, what will be the status of ʿAbdullāh ibn Judʿān in the Hereafter?"

The Prophet ﷺ said, "He will be in the Fire."

"But why?" she asked.

"Because not once in his life did he say, 'O Allāh, forgive me!'"

The Prophet ﷺ did not deny the virtue of ʿAbdullāh ibn Judʿān. He only referred to God's command that righteous actions in themselves cannot save a person in the Hereafter unless he believes in God and performs actions that please Him. Islam teaches that God will reward a disbeliever for their good deeds in this world, but there will be no reward for them in the afterlife.

The things of this transient world, including faith and heart, require constant care to work optimally. For example, when moving parts wear out after prolonged use, we lubricate them to run smoothly.

The Prophet Muhammad ﷺ said, "Verily, one's faith wears out, just as a shirt becomes worn out, so ask Allāh to renew faith in your hearts."[371] Even as a messenger of Allāh, the Prophet ﷺ frequently implored His Lord to maintain a steadfast faith in his heart. This supplication implies that even the Prophet's ﷺ heart depended on God's help to remain positive and that his righteousness alone was not enough. Another wisdom we may deduce from this prayer is that Satan never stops casting his whispers no matter how often we repulse his attacks. He is an enemy against whom we must never lower our guard.

We learn from the Qur'ān and Sunnah[372] that our hearts become tranquil when we remember Allāh and agitated and rebellious when we forget Him. When we remember God, we become connected with Him, and that connection revives our hearts.

---

371. Mustadrak of al-Hākim, Ḥadīth #26.

372. Sunnah is the sayings, actions, and approvals of the Prophet Muhammad, and it includes the Ḥadīth (his sayings).

The reality is that most of us work on the physical heart and ignore its core, which is the fountain of faith and spirituality. Attending to the physical heart's needs is essential because it leads to good health, but rejuvenating the spiritual heart is indispensable because it guides us to positive actions and everlasting success.

Remembering God is the panacea for an ailing, erring, and rebellious heart. *Remembrance* is an overarching term that includes reciting the Qur'ān and, by extension, every action that follows Allāh's commandments concerning what is lawful and what is prohibited (ḥalāl and ḥarām, respectively). Ibn Taymiyyah said, "When the believer is engaged in *dhīkr* (God's remembrance), he is in reality connected to God. As long as one remains constantly connected to God, He will free the person from internal or external spiritual harm."[373]

When such a heart errs, it remediates by doing something positive because the Qur'ān says, *"Indeed, good deeds cancel out bad deeds."*[374] Satan tries to push us into despair that God will never forgive us for our sins. This verse forever throws a lifeline to us and dejects Satan. In other verses, Allāh urges us not to lose hope in His mercy and reminds us that He is Ever-Forgiving. Even if we forget to cancel out our evil deeds with good ones, beseeching God for forgiveness is another avenue to make things right.

---

373. Ahmad Ibn Taymiyyah, *Diseases of the Hearts and Their Cures*, trans. Abu Rumaysah. (Birmingham, UK: Dar-us-Sunnah, 2000). This work resulted from a class the author taught in Hayward, CA, in 1999.

374. Qur'ān 11:114.

In an immensely hopeful verse, Allāh ordered the Prophet Muhammad ﷺ to tell the people that their Lord is close to them and hears their invocations.

"And when My servants ask you [O Muhammad] about Me, tell them, I am indeed near. I respond to every supplicant's invocations when he calls on Me. So let them obey Me and believe in Me, so that they may be led aright." [375]

When we supplicate to God, the Creator of all things, we admit His Lordship and our servitude. We accept that only He can deliver us from our sins. Even more profound, the prayer illustrates that we seek refuge in God's mercy when we displease Him. In other words, no one can aid us against God. The Prophet Muhammad ﷺ used to pray, "There is no fleeing from You, and there is no place of protection and safety except with You O Allāh!"[376]

Revival of the heart requires self-reproach and humility. Looking inward for our faults is a medicine we all need. It would remove the self-righteousness that afflicts many of our hearts. If we think of ourselves as learned, think of how much we do not know. If being wealthy makes us arrogant, know that there is someone wealthier. If self-pride permeates our thinking, let's remember that the noblest in God's sight are those who are most God-conscious (49:13). If the feeling of racial superiority invades our hearts, know that there is only one race, the human race.

---

375. Qur'ān 2:186.

376. Bukhari, Vol. 1, Book 4, Ḥadīth #247.

A spiritual heart draws strength from a strong faith (*īmān*), which requires conviction. This conviction comes after a believer passes many trials and tribulations. In Islam, faith has three levels. The first is to become a "*Muslim*" (submitter) upon reciting the testimony of faith: "There is no god, but God; And Muhammad is the Messenger of God." The second is when a "*Muslim*" becomes a "*Mu'min*" (literally a believer), and the third is when a "*Mu'min*" excels in faith and becomes a "*Muḥsin.*"

The Qur'ān relates the story of a group of Bedouins who had newly converted to the faith (become *Muslim*). The new converts demanded certain privileges from the Prophet ﷺ that he had granted to early believers who had sacrificed much for faith, claiming they, too, were *Mu'mins.* God rejected their claim, saying they were only *Muslims* because, at this moment in time, their hearts still lacked the conviction of faith.[377] The incident points out that moving up the ladder is a slow process and does not come without perseverance in righteous actions and sacrifices. Just like one must show an achievement to deserve a promotion at work, a servant also needs to do meritorious deeds for God to raise his rank.

It is appropriate to conclude this book with a reminder about the centrality of our spiritual hearts. Nothing of our being is more important than the heart, and nothing requires more attention than it. The spiritual heart is the essence of our inner self, an organ that *thinks*, *sees*, *perceives*, and *remembers*. It is the repository of faith, God-consciousness, morality, and intentions.

377. Qur'ān 49:14.

Those who have sinned—and who haven't?—should not despair. Instead, we can revive our spiritual hearts by reconnecting with the heart's Creator. Given that God—the Most Patient (*Aṣ-Ṣabūr*)— does not immediately destroy us due to our sins could mean that He will accept us in His merciful embrace if we return to Him in repentance. It may also be a sign that He has not given up on us. Why would we give up on Him then? No matter how overwhelmed we might feel under the burden of sin, He can lift us and restore us to goodness.

As Rumi, the poet, said, "When the world pushes you to your knees, you're in the perfect position to pray."[378]

---

378. A famous aphorism of the 13th-century Persian poet Jalāl ad-Dīn Mohammad Rūmī.

Heart verses in the Qur'ān

Qalb/Qūlūb

Chapter	Verse
Al-Baqarah–2/The Cow	7, 10, 74, 88, 93, 97, 118, 204, 225, 260, 283
Āli ʿImrān-3/ The Family of ʿImrān	7, 8, 103, 126, 151, 154, 156, 159, 168
An-Nisā'-4/Women	63, 155
Al-Mā'idah-5/The Table Spread	13, 41, 52, 113
Al-Anʿām-6/Cattle	25, 43, 46
Al-Āʿrāf-7/The Heights	100, 101, 179
Al-Anfāl-8/Spoils of War	2, 10, 11, 12, 24, 49, 63, 70
At-Tawbah-9/Repentance	8, 45, 60, 64, 77, 87, 93, 110, 117, 125, 127
Yūnūs-10/Jonah	74, 88
Ar-Raʿd-13/Thunder	28
Al-Ḥījr-15/The Stone Valley	12
An-Naḥl-16/Bees	22, 106, 108
Al-Isra'-17/The Night Journey	46
Al-Kahf-18/The Cave	14, 28, 57
Al-Anbiyā'-21/The Prophets	30
Al-Ḥajj-22/The Pilgrimage	32, 35, 46, 53, 54

Al-Mū'minūn-23/The Believers	60, 63
An-Nūr-24/The Light	37, 50
Ash-Shū'arā-26/The Poets	89, 194, 200
Al-Qaṣaṣ-28/The Stories	10
Ar-Rūm-30/The Romans	59
Al-Aḥzāb-33/The Enemy Alliance	4, 5, 10, 12, 26, 32, 51, 53, 60
Saba'-34/Sheba	23
As-Ṣāffāt-37/The Angels in Ranks	83
Az-Zumar-39/The Successive Groups	22, 23, 45
Al-Ghāfir-40/The Forgiver	18, 35
Fuṣṣilat-41/Verses Well Explained	50
Ash-Shūra-42/Consultation	24
Al-Jāthiyah-45/The Kneeling	23
Muḥammad-47	16, 20, 24, 29
Al-Fatḥ-48/The Victory	4, 11, 12, 18, 26
Al-Ḥūjūrāt-49/The Private Quarters	3, 7, 14
Qāf-50	33, 37
Al-Ḥadīd-57/Iron	16, 27
Al-Mujādalah-58/The Pleading Woman	22
Al-Ḥashr-59/The Gathering	2, 10, 14
As-Ṣaff-61/The Solid Ranks	5

Al-Munāfiqūn-63/The Hypocrites	3
Al-Taghābūn-64/Mutual Loss and Gain	11
At-Tahrīm-66/The Prohibition	4
Al-Muddaththīr-74/The One Covered Up	31
Al-Nazi'āt-79/Angels Who Remove Souls	8
Al-Muṭaffifin-83/Defrauders	14

Ṣadr/Ṣūdūr

Chapter	Verse
Āli 'Imrān-3/ The Family of 'Imrān	29, 118, 119, 154
An-Nisā'-4/Women	90
Al-Mā'idah-5/The Table Spread	7
Al-An'ām-6/Cattle	125
Al-Ā'rāf-7/The Heights	2, 43
Al-Anfāl-8/Spoils of War	43
At-Tawbah-9/Repentance	14
Yūnūs-10/Jonah	57
Hūd-11	12, 50
Al-Ḥījr-15/The Stone Valley	47, 95
An-Naḥl-16/The Bee	106
Al-Isra'-17/The Night Journey	51

Ṭā-Hā - 20	25
Al-Ḥajj-22/The Pilgrimage	46
Ash-Shūʿarā-26/The Poets	13
An-Naml-27/The Ants	74
Al-Qaṣaṣ-28/The Stories	23, 69
Al-ʿAnkabūt-29/The Spider	10, 49
Luqmān-31	23
Fāṭīr-35/The Originator	38
Az-Zumar-39/The Successive Groups	7, 22
Al-Ghāfir-40/The Forgiver	19, 56, 80
Ash-Shūra-42/Consultation	24
Al-Ḥadīd-57/Iron	6
Al-Ḥashr-59/The Gathering	9, 13
Al-Taghābūn-64/Mutual Loss and Gain	4
Al-Mūlk-67/The Dominion	13
Ash-Sharḥ-94/Uplifting the Heart	1
Az-Zalzalah-99/The Final Earthquake	6
Al- ʿĀdiyāt-100/The Galloping Horses	10
An-Nās-114/Humankind	5

Fu’ād/Af’īdah

Chapter	Verse
Al’An’ām-6/The Cattle	110
Hūd-11	120
An-Naḥl-16/The Bee	78
Al-Isra’-17/The Night Journey	36
Almu’mīnūn-23/The Believers	78
Al-Fūrqān-25/The Criterion	32
Al-Qaṣaṣ-28/The Stories	10
As-Sajdah-32/The Prostration	9
An-Najm-53/The Stars	11
Al-Mulk-67/The Dominion	23

Bibliography

The Clear Qur'ān, trans. Mustafa Khaṭṭāb, (FIQE, Lombard, IL: 2016)

Bible, different translations.

Hadith from various collections:

An-Nawawi's 40 Ḥadīth

Bukhārī

Dārimī

Muwaṭṭā

Mu'jam al-Awsaṭ

Mukhtasar Shu'ab Al-Iman lil Bayhaqi

Muslim

Musnad Abu Ya'la

Musnad al-Shāmiyyīn

Mustadrak of al-Hākim

Rawḍat al-'Uqalā

Sunan Ahmad

Sunan ibn Majah

Tirmidhi

Ḥilyat al-Awliyā' – sayings of pious people

Siyar A'lām al-Nubalā, biography.

Books, Articles

A History of the Heart, Standford.edu, last accessed March 23, 2021, https://web.stanford.edu/class/history13/earlysciencelab/body/heartpages/heart.html.

A. Helwa, *Secrets of Divine Love: A Spiritual Journey into the Heart of Islam.* (Nanuet, NY: Naulit Publishing, 2020), 12.

Abu 'l-Hasan 'Ali al-Nadwi, "Shaykh Sayyid 'Abd al-Qadir al-Jilani," Hayat al-Ulama', January 17, 2013, last accessed March 23, 2021, https://hayatalulama.wordpress.com/2013/01/17/shaykh-sayyid-abd-al-qadir-al-jilani/.

Abū Bakr Aḥmad Ibn al-Ḥusayn al-Bayhaqī (d. 485 H), *Kitāb al-Zuhd al-kabīr*, ed. 'Āmir Aḥmad Ḥaydar, (Beirut: Mu'assasat al-Kutub al-Thaqāfiya, 1996), 165, no. 373.

Abu Hāmid Muhammad al-Ghazālī as quoted in *Ihya Ulum al-Din, Kitab Sharh 'Ajā'ib al-Qalb*, translated as *The Marvels of the Heart*, trans. Walter James Skellie. (Louisville: Fons Vitae, 2010), 28.

Ahmad Ibn Taymiyyah, *Diseases of the Hearts and Their Cures*, trans. Abu Rumaysah. (Birmingham, UK: Dar-us-Sunnah, 2000), 41.

Ahmad Ibn Taymiyyah, *Diseases of the Hearts and Their Cures*, trans. Abu Rumaysah. (Birmingham, UK: Dar-us-Sunnah, 2000). The author's full name was Taqī ad-Dīn Aḥmad ibn Abd al-Halim ibn Abd al-Salam al-Numayri al- Ḥarrānī.

Alcohol Abuse in the United States, National Institute on Alcohol Abuse and Alcoholism, last accessed March 23, 2021, www.niaaa.nih.gov/publications/brochures-and-fact-sheets/alcohol-facts-and-statistics.

Al-Dā' wa al-Dawā', *The Illness and Medicine*. (al-Mansoura, Egypt: Dar Al-Manarah, 2010), 42. See also Yasir Qadhi, Duʿā, *The Weapon of the Believer*. (Birmingham, UK: Al-Hidaayah Publishing and Distribution Ltd, 2003), 51.

Al-Jawziyyah, Ibn al-Qayyim, Zād al-Maʿād fī Hadyi Khayr al-ʿIbād. Eds. Shuʿaib al-Arnaʾūṭ and ʿAbd al-Qādir al-Arnaʾūṭ. Trans. by Mikail ibn Mahboob Ariff (Beirut: Muʾassasah al-Risālah, 1998), 24–25.

Amatullah, "The Heart: Fu'aad, Qalb and Sadr," Muslim Matters, Feb. 11, 2009, last accessed March 23, 2021, https://muslimmatters.org/2009/02/11/the-heart-fuaad-qalb-and-sadr/.

Amazing Heart Facts, Nova Online, last accessed March 21, 2021, https://www.pbs.org/wgbh/nova/heart/heartfacts.html.

American Life League, "The Harmful Effects of Pornography," EWTN.com, last accessed March 23, 2021, https://www.ewtn.com/catholicism/library/harmful-effects-of-pornography-9664.

Anger – how it affects people, Better Health Channel, last accessed March 23, 2021, https://www.betterhealth.vic.gov.au/health/healthyliving/anger-how-it-affects-people.

D. Bohm and B. J. Hiley, *The Undivided Universe* (London: Routledge: 1993).

D. S. Goldstein, "Stress, allostatic load, catecholamines, and other neurotransmitters in neurodegenerative diseases," *Cellular Molecular Neurobiology*, vol. 32, no. 5 (2011): 661–666. See also M. Frese, "Stress at work and psychosomatic complaints: a causal interpretation," *Journal of Applied Psychology*, vol. 70, no. 2 (1985): 314; J. Gaines and J. Jermier, "Emotional exhaustion in a high stress organization," *Academy of Management Journal*, vol. 26, no. 4 (1983): 567–586; and B. Fowers, "Perceived control, illness status, stress and adjustment to cardiac illness," *Journal of Psychology*, vol. 128, no. 5 (1994): 567–579.

D. T. Lunde, "Psychiatric complications of heart transplants," *American Journal of Psychiatry*, vol. 126, no. 3 (1969): 1190–1195. See also W. F. Kuhn et al., "Psychopathology in heart transplant candidates," *Journal of Heart Transplants,* vol. 7, no. 3 (1988): 223–226 and F. M. Mai, "Graft and donor denial in heart transplant recipients," *American Journal of Psychiatry*, vol. 143, no. 9 (1986): 1159–1161.

Earlexia Norwood, "Surprising Health Benefits of Smiling," http://www.henryfordlivewell.com/health-benefits-smiling.

Exploring the role of the heart in human performance, https://www.heartmath.org/research/science-of-the-heart/.

Farid al-Din Attar, Muslim Saints and Mystics: Episodes from the Tadhkirat al-Auliya' (Memorial of the Saints), transl. A.J. Arberry (Chicago, IL: University of Chicago Press, 1966), 51.

Feifei Sun, "Financial Suicides," *Vanity Fair* (April 2009), https://www.vanityfair.com/news/2009/04/financial-suicides.

G. E. Schwartz, L. G. Russek, "Dynamical energy systems and modern physics: Fostering the science and spirit of complementary and alternative medicine," *Alternative Therapies in Health Medicine*, vol. 3, no. 3 (1997):46–56. See also G. E. Schwartz, L. G. Russek, "Do all dynamical systems have memory? Implications of the systemic memory hypothesis for science and society," in *Brain and Values: Is a Biological Science of Values Possible?*, ed. K. H. Pribram. (Hillsdale, NJ: Lawrence Erlbaum Associates, 1998) and G. E. R. Schwartz, L. G. Russek, "The origin of holism and memory in nature: The systemic memory hypothesis," *Frontier Perspectives*, vol. 7, no. 2 (1998): 23–30.

G. Telegdy, G., "The action of ANP, BNP and related peptides on motivated behavior in rats," *Reviews in the Neurosciences*, vol. 5, no. 4 (1994): 309–315. See also J. Gutkowska, J., et al., "Oxytocin is a cardiovascular hormone," *Brazilian Journal of Medical and Biological Research*, vol. 33, n. 6 (2000): 625–633.

Ḥārith al-Muḥāsībī, Risāla al-Mustarshīdīn (Treatise for the Seekers of Guidance) transl. Zaid Shakir (Hayward, CA: NID Publishers, 2008), 91.

Harold G. Koenig, "Research on Religion, Spirituality and Mental Health: A Review," *Canadian Journal of Psychiatry* (2008).

Henry David Thoreau, "On the Art of writing," American Transcendentalilst Web, last accessed March 23, 2021, https://archive.vcu.edu/english/engweb/transcendentalism/authors/thoreau/hdt-art.html.

Ibn Abi al-Duniya in Makā'd al-Shaytān 60/39, quoted in *The Devil's Deceptions* by Imam ibn al-Jawzi, a translation of *Talbīs Iblīs* (Birmingham, UK: Dar as-Sunnah Publishers, 2014) 76.

Ibn Hajar al-Haythami, Fatāwa al-Kubra al-Fiqhīyyah, Dar Sader, Beirut.

Imam ibn al-Jawzi, 70. Footnote 87, p 28

Imam Ibnul Qayyim Al-Jawziyyah, *Spiritual Disease and Its Cure*. (London: Darussalam), 58–59.

Imamal Matharat al-Qulūb, *Purification of the Heart*, trans. Hamza Yusuf. (London: Dar Al Taqwa, 2020), 13.

In Islam, jinns are invisible creatures, like angels. While God created angels from light, He created jinns from a smokeless fire. Another quality that separates jinns from angels is that they have free will, like humans.

J. G. Miller, *Living Systems*. (New York, NY: McGraw-Hill, 1978).

J. Richard Jennings and Michael G.H. Coles, John I. Lacey, A Biographical Memoir, Biographical Memoirs, vol. 88 (Washington, DC: National Academy of Sciences, 2006).

Jenny Popplewell, *American Murder: The Family Next Door*, directed by Jenny Popplewell (2020; Los Angeles: Netflix).

K. H. Pribram, *Brain and Perception: Holonomy and Structure in Figural Processing* (Hillsdale, NJ: Lawrence Erlbaum Associates, Publishers, 1991). See also E. Laszlo, *Quantum Shift in the Global Brain: How the New Scientific Reality Can Change Us and Our World*. (Rochester, VT: Inner Traditions, 2008); E. Mitchell, Quantum holography: a basis for the interface between mind and matter, in *Bioelectromagnetic Medicine*, ed. P.G. Rosch and M.S. Markov (New York: Dekker, 2004): 153–158; W. A. Tiller, J. W. E. Dibble, and M. J. Kohane, *Conscious Acts of Creation: The Emergence of a New Physics*. (Walnut Creek, CA: Pavior Publishing, 2001): 201–202.

Kitāb al-Zuhd Kabir, ed. Muḥammad ʿAbd al-Salām Shāhīn (Beirut: Dār al-Kutub al-ʿIlmiyya, 1999), 99, no. 633.

M. A. Mittleman, et al., "Triggering of acute myocardial infarction onset by episodes of anger. Determinants of Myocardial Infarction Onset Study Investigators," *Circulation*, vol. 92, no. 7 (1995): 1720–1725.

Michael T. Murray, ND, and Joseph Pizzorno, ND, *The Encyclopedia of Natural Medicine*, (New York: Atria, 2012), 22.

Michael T. Murray, *What the Drug Companies Won't Tell You and Your Doctor Doesn't Know*. (New York: Simon & Schuster, 2009), 33.

Muhammad al-Kharraz al-Baghdadi (d. 277 or 286 AH) was a famous mystic. Quoted by Al-Ghazāli in *Ihya Ulum al-Din, Kitab Sharh 'Ajā'ib al-Qalb*, translated as *The Marvels of the Heart*, trans. Walter James Skellie. (Louisville: Fons Vitae, 2010), 107.

Muhammad Ibn Ishāq, Sirāt Rasūl Allāh, *The Life of Muhammad*, 27th ed., trans. A. Guillaume. (Karachi: Oxford University Press, 2014), 193.

Organ Transplants and Cellular Memories, Paul.Pearsall.com, last accessed March 23, 2021, https://www.paulpearsall.com/info/press/3.html.

Porn Harms, Endsexualexploitation.org, last accessed March 23, 2021, https://endsexualexploitation.org/pornography/.

Quran Dictionary, Corpus Quran, last accessed March 23, 2021, http://corpus.quran.com/qurandictionary.jsp?q=*kr. This is an open-source project. The Quranic Arabic Corpus is available under the GNU public license with terms of use.

Related by Imām al-Qurtubī in al-Tadkhīra, according to American scholar Suhaib Webb.

Reported by Imam Ahmad in "Fadā'il Al-Sahābah," Abu Nu`aym in "Dalā'il Al-Nubuwwah," Al-Diya' in his "Al-Muntaqa min Al-Masmu`at", Ibn 'Asākir in his "Tārīkh," Al-Bayhaqy in "Dalā'il Al-Nubuwwah," and Ibn Hajar in "Al-Isābah" with a good chain of narration.

Rollin McCraty, *Science of the Heart: Exploring the Role of the Heart in Human Performance*, vol. 2 (Boulder Creek, CA: HeartMath Institute, 2015), 2.

Rollin McCraty, Science of the Heart: Exploring the Role of the Heart in Human Performance, vol. 2 (Boulder Creek, CA: HeartMath Institute, 2015), 5.

Rollin McCraty, Science of the Heart: Exploring the Role of the Heart in Human Performance, vol. 2 (Boulder Creek, CA: HeartMath Institute, 2015), 5.

Sharh as-mā al-Husnā (Explanation of Allah's Beautiful Names), vol. 2. (Karachi: Pakistan, House of Knowledge Trust, 2009), 24.

Sidi Abdullah Anik Misra, "What is the Difference Between the 'Heart' (Qalb), 'Kindling Heart' (fuaad), and the 'Pure Intellect' (lubb)?", Seekers Guidance, Nov. 4, 2009, last accessed March 23, 2021, https://seekersguidance.org/answers/general-counsel/what-is-the-difference-between-the-heart-qalb-kindling-heart-fuaad-and-the-pure-intellect-lubb/.

Smoking & Tobacco Use, Centers for Disease Control and Prevention, last accessed March 23, 2021, www.cdc.gov/tobacco/data_statistics/fact_sheets/fast_facts/index.htm#beginning.

Stephen Harrod Buhner, *The Intelligence of the Heart in the Direction Perception of Nature (The Secret Teachings of Plants)* (Rochester, VT: Bear & Company, 2004), 118.

Stephen Harrod Buhner, *The Intelligence of the Heart in the Direction Perception of Nature (The Secret Teachings of Plants)*. (Rochester, VT: Bear & Company, 2004): 91.

Tafsir ibn Kathir, abridged, vol. 6, trans. Safiur Rahman al-Mubarakpuri (Riyadh: Darussalam, 2000)

Tafsir Ibn Kathīr, abridged, vol. 6, trans. Safiur Rahmān Mubārakpurī. (Riyadh: Darussalam, 2000), 688.

The human heart in the glorious Quran, The Quran Project, last accessed March 23, 2021, http://quranproject.org/The-human-heart-in-the-glorious-Quran-481-d. See also https://tanzil.net/.

The proper name for the Only Creator and the Supreme Being in the Arabic language is Allāh. Muslims believe that only the word Allāh encompasses the unique qualities of the Creator. Like Muslims, Arab Christians also refer to the Creator as Allāh. In this book, the author uses Allāh and God interchangeably to help Western readers, mindful that the term "God" is limited in its meaning.

The quote, attributed to Mary Stevenson, has been modified and abridged. For the original version see https://www.footprints-inthe-sand.com/index.php?page=Bio.php.

Thupten Jinpa, *A Fearless Heart: How the Courage to Become Compassionate Can Transform Our Lives*. (New York: Avery, 2015), 124.

Underlying Causes of Death, 1999–2019, Centers for Disease Control and Prevention, last accessed March 23, 2021, https://wonder.cdc.gov/ucd-icd10.html.

Where are memories stored in the brain?, Queensland Brain Institute, last accessed March 23, 2021, https://qbi.uq.edu.au/brain-basics/memory/where-are-memories-stored.

William Knox, *Poets.org*, last accessed March 23, 2021, https://poets.org/poet/william-knox.

World TB Day 2020, Centers for Disease Control and Prevention, last accessed March 23, 2021, https://www.cdc.gov/tb/worldtbday/history.htm.

Glossary

Arabic Terms	English Translation
'Abbās	The strongest lion
'Ād	A previous nation in Arabia
'Amal ṣāleḥ	Righteous actions
'Ilm	Knowledge
'Ēsa	Jesus
Ādam	Adam, first man and prophet
'Ajam (dumb).	Dumb/mute
Al-Asmā al-Ḥusna	The best names
Al-fahshā	Indecency
Al-Furqān	The Criterion
Al-Ghafūr	The Ever-Forgiving
Al-Hādi	The Guide
Allāh	The One Supreme God
Al-Mu'min	The Bestower of Faith, believer
Al-muttaqūn	The pious, righteous
Al-Raḥīm	The Especially Merciful
Al-Raḥmān	The Universally Merciful
Al-Ṣamad	The Self-Sufficient, Besought
Al-Ṭayyab	Good, pure
Al-Wahhāb	The Bestower
Anṣār	The helpers of Medina
Asad,	A brave and fearless lion

Awli'yā	Pious people
Ayyūb	A prophet
Ba'īd	Far, or nearly impossible
Bahnas,	A prancing lion
Bāsil,	A fierce lion
Dāwūd	David
Dhi al-Ṭhawl	The Owner of Abundance
Dhīkr	Reminder/mention
Dhul Hījjah	Last (12th) month of the Islamic calendar
Du'ā	Supplication
Faqīr	Needy, beggar
Fawzun'adhīm	Ultimate triumph
Fīr'awn	Pharaoh
Firāsah	Intuition
Fiṭrah	Innate nature
Fu'ād	Inflamed heart
Ghaflah	Heedlessness
Ghībah	Backbiting
Ghīrah	Protective jealously
Hābīl	Abel
Ḥadīth	Statements of the Prophet Muhammad
Hajj	Pilgrimage
Ḥalāl	Lawful
Ḥamd	Praise
Ḥarām	Prohibited
Ḥasad	Envy

Ḥaydar	A plump lion
Ḥikmah	Wisdom
Hūd	Eber
Ḥuffāẓ (sing. ḥāfiẓ)	One who memorized the entire Qur'ān
Iblīs	Despondent/Satan
Ibn Sina	Avicenna
Ibrāhīm	Abraham
Ikhlās	Sincerity
Īmān	Faith
Insān	Human
Ismā'īl	Ishmael
Janīn	Fetus
Jannah	Paradise
Jibrīl	Gabriel
Jihād Akbar	A bigger struggle
Jihād Asghar	A lesser struggle
Jinn	An invisible creature God created from the flames of "smokeless fire
Karāmah	Spiritual marvels of the pious
Khalīl	Close friend
Khashī'ah	Fear, awe
Kitāb al-Riqāq	Book of Softening of the Heart
Kufr	Disbelief
Madinah	Medina
Makkah	Mecca
Maqluba	Arabic dish/something upside down
Mīḥrāb	Niche

Mu‘allaqāt	The hanging ones; refers to the seven poems hung from the door of the Ka'bah.
Muhājirūn	The Emigrants from Mecca
Mu‘jizah	Miracle
Munāfiqūn	The hypocrites
Musā	Moses
Nafs	Self
Nafs al-lawwāmah	A self that reproaches a sinner
Nafs al-muṭma'innah	A tranquil self that is content with God's decree in all circumstances
Nafs-al-'ammārah,	The lower self that pushes toward sin
Nūh	Noah
Oyūb	Blemishes, defects
Qābīl	Cain
Qadr	Predestiny
Qalb	Heart
Qalbun munīb	Self-reproaching heart
Qalbun salīm	A pure, sound heart
Qarīn	Angel or devil companion
Qārūn	Korah
Qasam	An oath
Qīṣās	"Life for a life," equality in punishment
Rajā	Hope
Ri'ya	Ostentatiousness, show off
Rūḥ	Soul, spirit
Sābiqū)	To compete
Ṣābirūn	The patient

Ṣadr	Chest, heart's external covering
Salām	Peace (greeting of)
Ṣalāt al-Istīikhārah,	The prayer of seeking counsel
Ṣāleḥ	Shelah
Sāriʿū	To hasten
Sayyid al-Istīghfār:	Master supplication
Shahawāt	Desires, lusts
Shahīd	Martyr
Shayṭān	Satan, devil
Shayṭanah	Something far
Shibl	A cub lion
Shirk	Polytheism
Shūbūhāt	Doubts
Shukr	Thanks
Sunnah	Prophet Muhammad's actions, sayings, and approvals
Surah	Chapter of the Qur'ān
Tafakkūr	Contemplation
Tahajjud	Late-night prayer
Targhīb	Encouragement
Tarhīb	Threat, warning
Taṭhīr qalb	Purification of the heart
Tawakkūl	Putting one's trust in Allāh
Tawassul	Intermediation
Tazkiyatun nafs	The purification of the self
Thamūd	An ancient nation in Arabia
Waḥy	Revelation

Yā'qūb	Jacob
Yaḥyā	John the Baptist
Yūnūs	Jonah
Zakariyya	Zechariah